W9-CFV-532

WITHDRAWN

SOUTHEAST AFRICA

SOUTHEAST AFRICA

1880 TO THE PRESENT:
RECLAIMING A REGION OF NATURAL WEALTH

DANIEL E. HARMON

INTRODUCTORY ESSAY BY
Dr. Richard E. Leakey
Chairman, Wildlife Clubs
of Kenya Association
⁘

AFTERWORD BY
Deirdre Shields

CHELSEA HOUSE PUBLISHERS
Philadelphia
In association with Covos Day Books, South Africa

CHELSEA HOUSE PUBLISHERS

EDITOR IN CHIEF Sally Cheney
DIRECTOR OF PRODUCTION Kim Shinners
CREATIVE MANAGER Takeshi Takahashi
MANUFACTURING MANAGER Diann Grasse
SERIES DESIGNER Keith Trego
COVER DESIGN Emiliano Begnardi

The Chelsea House World Wide Web address is http://www.chelseahouse.com

First Printing

1 3 5 7 9 8 6 4 2

Library of Congress Cataloging-in-Publication Data

Harmon, Daniel E.
    Southeast Africa: 1880 to the present : reclaiming a region of natural wealth / Daniel E.
Harmon; introductory essay by Richard E. Leakey ; afterword by Deirdre Shields.
       p. cm. — (Exploration of Africa, the emerging nations)
    Includes bibliographical references and index.
    ISBN 0-7910-5747-X (alk. paper)
    1. Africa, Southern—History. 2. Zimbabwe—History. 3. Zambia—History. 4.
    Malawi—History. 5. Mozambique—History. 6. Madagascar—History. I. Leakey, Richard
    E. II. Title. III. Exploration of Africa, the emerging nations.

DT1079 .H37 2002
968—dc21

                                                          2001055282

The photographs in this book are from the Royal Geographical Society Picture Library. Most are being published for the first time.

The Royal Geographical Society Picture Library provides an unrivaled source of over half a million images of
peoples and landscapes from around the globe. Photographs date from the 1840s onwards on a variety of sub-
jects including the British Colonial Empire, deserts, exploration, indigenous peoples, landscapes, remote desti-
nations, and travel.

Photography, beginning with the daguerreotype in 1839, is only marginally younger than the Society, which
encouraged its explorers to use the new medium from its earliest days. From the remarkable mid-19th century
black-and-white photographs to color transparencies of the late 20th century, the focus of the collection is not the
generic stock shot but the portrayal of man's resilience, adaptability, and mobility in remote parts of the world.

In organizing this project, we have incurred many debts of gratitude. Our first, though, is to the professional staff
of the Picture Library for their generous assistance, especially to Joanna Scadden, Picture Library Manager.

CONTENTS

EXPLORATION OF AFRICA: THE EMERGING NATIONS

THE DARK CONTINENT

DR. RICHARD E. LEAKEY

THE CONCEPT OF AFRICAN exploration has been greatly influenced by the hero status given to the European adventurers and missionaries who went off to Africa in the last century. Their travels and travails were certainly extraordinary and nobody can help but be impressed by the tremendous physical and intellectual courage that was so much a characteristic of people such as Livingstone, Stanley, Speke, and Baker, to name just a few. The challenges and rewards that Africa offered, both in terms of commerce and also "saved souls," inspired people to take incredible risks and endure personal suffering to a degree that was probably unique to the exploration of Africa.

I myself was fortunate enough to have had the opportunity to organize one or two minor expeditions to remote spots in Africa where there were no roads or airfields and marching with porters and/or camels was the best option at the time. I have also had the thrill of being with people untouched and often unmoved by contact with Western or other technologically based cultures, and these experiences remain for me amongst the most exciting and salutary of my life. With the contemporary revolution in technology, there will be few if any such opportunities again. Indeed I often find myself slightly saddened by the realization that were life ever discovered on another planet, exploration would doubtless be done by remote sensing and making full use of artificial, digital intelligence. At least it is unlikely to be in my lifetime and this is a relief!

Notwithstanding all of this, I believe that the age of exploration and discovery in Africa is far from over. The future offers incredible opportunities for new discoveries that will push back the frontiers of knowledge. This endeavor will of course not involve exotic and arduous journeys into malaria-infested tropical swamps, but it will certainly require dedication, team work, public support, and a conviction that the rewards to be gained will more than justify the efforts and investment.

EARLY EXPLORERS

Many of us were raised and educated at school with the belief that Africa, the so-called Dark Continent, was actually discovered by early European travelers and explorers. The date of this "discovery" is difficult to establish, and anyway a distinction has always had to be drawn between northern Africa and the vast area south of the Sahara. The Romans certainly had information about the continent's interior as did others such as the Greeks. A diverse range of traders ventured down both the west coast and the east coast from at least the ninth century, and by the tenth century Islam had taken root in a number of new towns and settlements established by Persian and Arab interests along the eastern tropical shores. Trans-African trade was probably under way well before this time, perhaps partly stimulated by external interests.

Close to the beginning of the first millennium, early Christians were establishing the Coptic church in the ancient kingdom of Ethiopia and at other coastal settlements along Africa's northern Mediterranean coast. Along the west coast of Africa, European trade in gold, ivory, and people was well established by the sixteenth century. Several hundred years later, early in the 19th century, the systematic penetration and geographical exploration of Africa was undertaken by Europeans seeking geographical knowledge and territory and looking for opportunities not only for commerce but for the chance to spread the Gospel. The extraordinary narratives of some of the journeys of early European travelers and adventurers in Africa are a vivid reminder of just how recently Africa has become embroiled in the power struggles and vested interests of non-Africans.

THE DARK CONTINENT

AFRICA'S GIFT TO THE WORLD

My own preoccupation over the past thirty years has been to study human prehistory, and from this perspective it is very clear that Africa was never "discovered" in the sense in which so many people have been and, perhaps, still are being taught. Rather, it was Africans themselves who found that there was a world beyond their shores.

Prior to about two million years ago, the only humans or proto-humans in existence were confined to Africa; as yet, the remaining world had not been exposed to this strange mammalian species, which in time came to dominate the entire planet. It is no trivial matter to recognize the cultural implications that arise from this entirely different perspective of Africa and its relationship to the rest of humanity.

How many of the world's population grow up knowing that it was in fact African people who first moved and settled in southern Europe and Central Asia and migrated to the Far East? How many know that Africa's principal contribution to the world is in fact humanity itself? These concepts are quite different from the notion that Africa was only "discovered" in the past few hundred years and will surely change the commonly held idea that somehow Africa is a "laggard," late to come onto the world stage.

It could be argued that our early human forebears—the *Homo erectus* who moved out of Africa—have little or no bearing on the contemporary world and its problems. I disagree and believe that the often pejorative thoughts that are associated with the Dark Continent and dark skins, as well as with the general sense that Africans are somehow outside the mainstream of human achievement, would be entirely negated by the full acceptance of a universal African heritage for all of humanity. This, after all, is the truth that has now been firmly established by scientific inquiry.

The study of human origins and prehistory will surely continue to be important in a number of regions of Africa and this research must continue to rank high on the list of relevant ongoing exploration and discovery. There is still much to be learned about the early stages of human development, and the age of the "first humans"—the first bipedal apes—has not been firmly established. The current hypothesis is that prior to five million years ago there were no bipeds, and this would mean that humankind is only five million years old. Beyond Africa, there were no humans until just two million years ago, and this is a consideration that political leaders and people as a whole need to bear in mind.

RECENT HISTORY

When it comes to the relatively recent history of Africa's contemporary people, there is still considerable ignorance. The evidence suggests that there were major migrations of people within the continent during the past 5,000 years, and the impact of the introduction of domestic stock must have been quite considerable on the way of life of many of Africa's people. Early settlements and the beginnings of nation states are, as yet, poorly researched and recorded. Although archaeological studies have been undertaken in Africa for well over a hundred years, there remain more questions than answers.

One question of universal interest concerns the origin and inspiration for the civilization of early Egypt. The Nile has, of course, offered opportunities for contacts between the heart of Africa and the Mediterranean seacoast, but very little is known about human settlement and civilization in the upper reaches of the Blue and White Nile between 4,000 and 10,000 years ago. We do know that the present Sahara Desert is only about 10,000 years old; before this Central Africa was wetter and more fertile, and research findings have shown that it was only during the past 10,000 years that Lake Turkana in the northern Kenya was isolated from the Nile system. When connected, it would have been an excellent connection between the heartland of the continent and the Mediterranean.

Another question focuses on the extensive stone-walled villages and towns in Southern Africa. The Great Zimbabwe is but one of thousands of standing monuments in East, Central, and Southern Africa that attest to considerable human endeavor in Africa long before contact with Europe or Arabia. The Neolithic period and Iron Age still offer very great opportunities for exploration and discovery.

As an example of the importance of history, let us look at the modern South Africa where a visitor might still be struck by the not-too-subtle representation of a past that, until a few years ago, only "began" with the arrival of Dutch settlers some 400 years back. There are, of course, many pre-Dutch sites, including extensive fortified towns where kingdoms and nation states had thrived hundreds of years before contact with Europe; but this evidence has been poorly documented and even more poorly portrayed.

Few need to be reminded of the sparseness of Africa's precolonial written history. There are countless cultures and historical narratives that have been recorded only as oral history and legend. As postcolonial Africa further consolidates itself, history must be reviewed and deepened to incorporate the realities of precolonial human settlement as well as foreign contact. Africa's identity and self-respect is closely linked to this.

One of the great tragedies is that African history was of little interest to the early European travelers who were in a hurry and had no brief to document the details of the people they came across during their travels. In the basements of countless European museums, there are stacked shelves of African "curios"—objects taken from the people but seldom documented in terms of the objects' use, customs, and history.

There is surely an opportunity here for contemporary scholars to do something. While much of Africa's precolonial past has been obscured by the slave trade, colonialism, evangelism, and modernization, there remains an opportunity, at least in some parts of the continent, to record what still exists. This has to be one of the most vital frontiers for African exploration and discovery as we approach the end of this millennium. Some of the work will require trips to the field, but great gains could be achieved by a systematic and coordinated effort to record the inventories of European museums and archives. The Royal Geographical Society could well play a leading role in this chapter of African exploration. The compilation of a central data bank on what is known and what exists would, if based on a coordinated initiative to record the customs and social organization of Africa's remaining indigenous peoples, be a huge contribution to the heritage of humankind.

MEDICINES AND FOODS

On the African continent itself, there remain countless other areas for exploration and discovery. Such endeavors will be achieved without the fanfare of great expeditions and high adventure as was the case during the last century and they should, as far as possible, involve exploration and discovery of African frontiers by Africans themselves. These frontiers are not geographic: they are boundaries of knowledge in the sphere of Africa's home-grown cultures and natural world.

Indigenous knowledge is a very poorly documented subject in many parts of the world, and Africa is a prime example of a continent where centuries of accumulated local knowledge is rapidly disappearing in the face of modernization. I believe, for example, that there is much to be learned about the use of wild African plants for both medicinal and nutritional purposes. Such knowledge, kept to a large extent as the experience and memory of elders in various indigenous communities, could potentially have far-reaching benefits for Africa and for humanity as a whole.

The importance of new remedies based on age-old medicines cannot be underestimated. Over the past two decades, international companies have begun to take note and to exploit certain African plants for pharmacological preparations. All too often, Africa has not been the beneficiary of these "discoveries," which are, in most instances, nothing more than the refinement and improvement of traditional African medicine. The opportunities for exploration and discovery in this area are immense and will have assured economic return on investment. One can only hope that such work will be in partnership with the people of Africa and not at the expense of the continent's best interests.

Within the same context, there is much to be learned about the traditional knowledge of the thousands of plants that have been utilized by different African communities for food. The contemporary world has become almost entirely dependent, in terms of staple foods, on the cultivation of only six principal plants: corn, wheat, rice, yams, potatoes, and bananas. This cannot be a secure basis to guarantee the food requirements of more than five billion people.

Many traditional food plants in Africa are drought resistant and might well offer new alternatives for large-scale agricultural development in the years to come. Crucial to this development is finding out what African people used before exotics were introduced. In some rural areas of the continent, it is still possible to learn about much of this by talking to the older generation. It is certainly a great shame that some of the early European travelers in Africa were ill equipped to study and record details of diet and traditional plant use, but I am sure that, although it is late, it is not too late. The compilation of a pan-African database on what is known about the use of the continent's plant resources is a vital matter requiring action.

VANISHING SPECIES

In the same spirit, there is as yet a very incomplete inventory of the continent's other species. The inevitable trend of bringing land into productive management is resulting in the loss of unknown but undoubtedly large numbers of species. This genetic resource may be invaluable to the future of Africa and indeed humankind, and there really is a need for coordinated efforts to record and understand the continent's biodiversity.

In recent years important advances have been made in the study of tropical ecosystems in Central and South America, and I am sure that similar endeavors in Africa would be rewarding. At present, Africa's semi-arid and highland ecosystems are better understood than the more diverse and complex lowland forests, which are themselves under particular threat from loggers and farmers. The challenges of exploring the biodiversity of the upper canopy in the tropical forests, using the same techniques that are now used in Central American forests, are fantastic and might also lead to eco-tourist developments for these areas in the future.

It is indeed an irony that huge amounts of money are being spent by the advanced nations in an effort to discover life beyond our own planet, while at the same time nobody on this planet knows the extent and variety of life here at home. The tropics are especially relevant in this regard and one can only hope that Africa will become the focus of renewed efforts of research on biodiversity and tropical ecology.

AN AFROCENTRIC VIEW

Overall, the history of Africa has been presented from an entirely Eurocentric or even Caucasocentric perspective, and until recently this has not been adequately reviewed. The penetration of Africa, especially during the last century, was important in its own way; but today the realities of African history, art, culture, and politics are better known. The time has come to regard African history in terms of what has happened in Africa itself, rather than simply in terms of what non-African individuals did when they first traveled to the continent.

INTRODUCTION

It must have been a startling and amusing sight for an American traveler in the African interior. Standing erect, proud, and authoritative at the intersection of dirt road and train track, the banded post topped by crossed boards expressed a familiar, unmistakable warning: STOP, LOOK, LISTEN—in the Bantu language. Beside it in the photograph, which appeared in a 1935 issue of *The National Geographic Magazine*, paused a vintage American sedan whose white-hatted driver gawked through an open window. To visiting foreigners, this was an unexpected yet indisputable sign of the times. "Civilization" had come to Rhodesia.

And in a mere half-century. Less than fifty years before, Cecil Rhodes—the shrewd British entrepreneur from whom the territory got its colonial name—had obtained a company charter from the government in London and pushed northward from England's South African anchor colony. His home country already had claimed strategic Cairo at the northern end of the continent, Cape Town at the southern tip. Now, Rhodes vowed, he would deliver a mineral-rich domain in the south-central interior to add to Britain's share of the African pie.

Zambian Man, c. 1920

Essentially, he did just that. With a comparative handful of whites, Rhodes and his successors established a strong mining-oriented colony that would outlast most of the other European regimes in Africa. In the process, they sowed seeds of bitterness that would end only after an extended season of violence and economic paralysis, long after most other colonial administrations had withdrawn.

But in 1935 Rhodesia—"The Pioneer Colony," as one chronicler described it—was at its peak of prosperity. Although Rhodes's British South Africa Company had been disbanded a dozen years earlier, his vision in large part had come to pass. Thousands of Africans were at work digging and shipping minerals, lining the pockets of colonial industrialists. They were growing millions of bushels of maize, wheat, citrus fruits, and other export crops annually.

Americans and other tourists came to enjoy the open space and the breathtaking sight of Victoria Falls, to drive the straight rural roads cut through giant anthills, to hunt big game, to wrestle ten-pound, sharp-toothed tiger fish from the River Zambezi. A typical journalist of the era recorded languidly, "Herds of eland, kudu, tsessebe (or sassaby), impala, and diminutive duikers detoured skittishly within a stone's throw of our car as we circled the roadless veld, following that most beautiful of sights, the 'dun deer' in his native haunts." Passing through the industrial areas, the visitors couldn't fail to observe the sharp discrepancies between living conditions of the African working class and the white administrative/management class. But for the most part, they weren't bothered by the situation. In some respects, the lot of the Africans here appeared far better than in other colonies.

UNIQUE ROADS THROUGH THE COLONIAL WILDERNESS

The modern-day countries of Southeast Africa emerged from very different colonial experiences, and they are today quite different from one another. Zambia and Zimbabwe (formerly Northern and Southern Rhodesia) came through the twentieth century under the rule of Great Britain, as did their neighbor Malawi. East of them, the coastal nation of Mozambique earned a life of its own after shaking off Portuguese domination. And off the coast, the large island of Madagascar became an independent nation in the aftermath of seventy years of French control. The colonial system was different for each of these European master countries, and the paths toward independence took different turns. Furthermore, the sovereign nations that were formed in the late 1900s adopted different forms of government and approaches to the formidable problems they faced, problems that were likewise different for each nation.

Bemba, Zambia, c. 1920 *Most Zambians are of Bantu origin. The complex patterns of immigration to the area have created wide linguistic and cultural differences. At least eighty languages or dialects are spoken in Zambia. The Bemba people account for more than a plurality of the population. Second in ranking are the Nyasja, and third are the Tonga.*

Non-Africans tend to live in towns. Many Europeans left at the time of independence (1964), and their numbers have steadily declined. By contrast, the number of Asians has risen, most of whom are involved in retail trade.

Coastland, Heartland

Vast coastal marshes; majestic highlands; broad, open *savannahs*; forests diverse in plant life; spectacular river gorges and waterfalls . . . This is the southeastern region of Africa. It's a scenic realm rich in wildlife, minerals, and beautiful vistas. And it's the domain of a hardy, fascinating people.

Southeast Africa, when you look at it on a map of the great continent, seems to be a region somewhat out of the way. Below it is the country of South Africa, whose *apartheid* policy and freedom struggle dominated African news coverage through much of the late twentieth century. Northward up the Indian Ocean coast lie Tanzania and Kenya, whose sweeping, wildlife-laden landscapes have inspired movies and nature documentaries. Less familiar in the world's eye, by comparison, are the countries in between.

In this study, we will learn about the region's mainland countries of Malawi, Mozambique, Zambia, and Zimbabwe, as well as Madagascar, the large island off Africa's southeastern coast.

Early Africans

Scientists believe Neanderthals, the prehistoric ancestors of humans, lived in Southeast Africa more than 200,000 years ago. By the Stone Age, some 15,000 years

The Peopling of Mozambique in the Precolonial Period

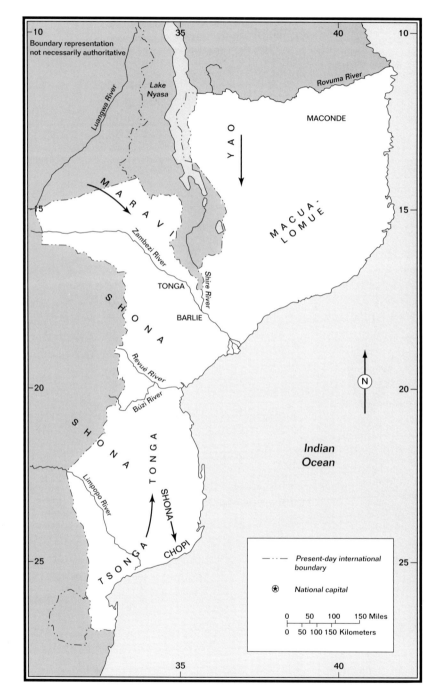

Boundary representation not necessarily authoritative

Luangwa River

Lake Nyasa

Rovuma River

MACONDE

Y A O

M A R A V I

Zambezi River

MACUA-LOMUE

TONGA

Shire River

BARLIE

S H O N A

Revuê River

Búzi River

S H O N A

Limpopo River

T O N G A

SHONA

CHOPI

T S O N G A

Indian Ocean

N

--- · — *Present-day international boundary*

✹ *National capital*

| 0 | 50 | 100 | 150 Miles |
| 0 | 50 | 100 | 150 Kilometers |

ago, wandering hunters who used early rock tools roamed the region. They included San bush dwellers, whose descendants make up a small part of the African population today.

Iron Age people of the Bantu tongue migrated southward from Central Africa almost 2,000 years ago. They farmed, herded cattle, and hunted for a living. They lived in thatch-roofed, earth-walled houses. In the farming villages of modern Zimbabwe you still see homes of this type. These newcomers made tools, weapons, fishhooks, and other items from iron and copper. They also were skilled potters.

Another Bantu migration came centuries later. Different peoples established small kingdoms in different parts of the region over the centuries. Sometimes they fought. The more powerful kings spread their domains to take in nearby villages, forcing the inhabitants to pay them *tribute*.

By the time of the early Bantu migration, eastern Africa already was the scene of intercontinental trade. Sailing vessels from India and Asia were bringing jewelry, cloth, and other goods to the African islands and coastal civilizations. They traded these for African goods—and human slaves.

When Europeans began exploring down the west coast of Africa in the 1400s, they established a similar trade network. Items of commerce were moving between the west coast and south-central Africa (modern-day Zambia) by the 1800s. The Portuguese and other Europeans took away slaves, ivory tusks, minerals, and other natural resources in exchange for products such as tools, jewelry, alcohol, and eventually firearms.

During the mid-1800s, Swahili-speaking Africans from the east coast traded extensively in the interior. They were joined by other native Africans from South Africa who fled the fierce Zulu activities in their homeland. Bantu descendants, however, remained the dominant population in Southeast Africa.

EUROPEANS ARRIVE ON THE EAST COAST

In 1488 Bartholomew Diaz of Portugal earned fame as the first European to round the Cape of Good Hope at the bottom of Africa and enter the Indian Ocean. At that time in history, Portugal was vying with Spain and other European powers to establish settlements and colonies in distant, unexplored lands. Portugal was first to enter the Indian Ocean and touch the eastern coast of Africa. But during the coming centuries, it would have to contend with the British, Dutch, and French in making actual claims.

Beginning in 1509, the Portuguese built trading ports on the coast of modern-day Mozambique and several hundred miles inland along the River Zambezi. They shipped ivory, slaves, and other cargo from this part of Africa. For decades after other European countries curtailed and eventually banned slave trading in the late eighteenth and early nineteenth centuries, the Portuguese still fostered slave raiding by native tribes throughout Southeast Africa. By the time slavery finally was abolished in the Portuguese colony of Brazil in 1888, Mozambique had become the leading supplier of African slaves for Caribbean and South American plantations.

For a while, some optimistic Portuguese believed they could forge a wide trading empire across the lower continent, from the Indian Ocean to the Atlantic. An expedition in 1798 failed when natives mounted formidable opposition and the Europeans' leader, scientist Francisco Lacerda, died of a jungle sickness. Portuguese explorers eventually made the Indian-Atlantic crossing, but the home country was too poor to take advantage of their efforts. By the late 1800s, any dreams of a coast-to-coast colony were erased by Great Britain's bold thrust into the lower continent's interior.

KEEPING AN EYE TURNED TOWARD THE SOUTH

The affairs of Southeast Africa, especially Zimbabwe and Mozambique, long have been linked with those of the Republic of South Africa. As mentioned above, South Africa has dominated news reports from the lower continent for the past fifty years. Even during colonial years and before, however, events in South Africa affected territories to the north.

South Africa was comparatively rich among the African colonies, thanks to its gold and other minerals. Mining developed quickly on a large scale during the late 1800s. It was such a prosperous and active industry that thousands of migrant laborers, willing to work for low wages, were hired from the colonies to the north. Some 80,000 laborers from the lower half of Mozambique would be among the foreigners at work in South Africa by 1936.

Throughout the colonial era, South Africa's northern neighbors were in what historian Richard W. Hull has termed "a dependent, satellite relationship to South Africa." In some ways, the region of Southeast Africa below the River Zambezi has had more in common with the Transvaal area of South Africa than with the territories north of the Zambezi. South Africa's economic influence has been felt in Zambia, Malawi, and beyond.

The region also contains large tracts of promising agricultural terrain. O. W. Barrett, a journalist visiting Mozambique in the early 1900s, wrote, "In the Zambezia district there has been spent a large amount of money in agricultural experiments, and, though the results are not encouraging thus far, it is no fault of the land. I have never seen any soils quite so rich, apparently, in either temperate or tropical America as are to be found in the Zambesi, Limpopo, and Inkomati alluvial plains."

The River Zambezi divides Zambia and Zimbabwe, then runs through the center of Mozambique on its way to the Indian Ocean. The Zambezi is a major African river, nourishing a lush valley. Before the Europeans arrived, the Shona empire controlled a brisk trade along the Zambezi. Ivory, copper, and slaves were sent downriver to the Indian Ocean to be exchanged for goods from Arabia and India.

MALAWI ON THE LAKE

As in other Southeast African regions, the Bantu migration beginning about 2,000 years ago was the major ancestral

Dugouts, Upper Zambezi River, c. 1903–1905 *The Zambezi River drains a large portion of south-central Africa. Together with its many tributaries, it forms the fourth largest river basin of the African continent. The river flows eastward for about 2,200 miles from its sources in central Africa, and it empties into the Indian Ocean. The Zambezi either crosses or forms the boundaries of six countries: Angola, Zambia, Namibia, Botswana, Zimbabwe, and Mozambique. The use of its waters has been the subject of numerous international agreements.*

Woman With Bible, Northern Rhodesia, c. 1910 *The first Christian missionaries arrived in Northern Rhodesia and other mainland countries, such as Malawi, before colonial rule. The explorer-missionary David Livingstone, who crossed Zambia during his three expeditions (1853–1873), inspired other missionaries to come to central Africa and continue his struggle against slavery and the slave trade.*

Today, Malawi and Zambia are predominantly Christian, including Roman Catholics, Anglicans, Baptists, Methodists, and other Christian denominations. The growth of independent churches, especially Jehovah's Witnesses, has occurred since independence (1964). There are relatively few Muslims in the African population.

influence on Malawi's population. The Malawi kingdom that gave the country its name was a powerful force in the area for more than three centuries beginning in the 1400s.

The Great Rift Valley of eastern Africa dominates Malawi's terrain. Lake Malawi (formerly called Lake Nyasa), with some 200 fish species, lies in the valley. On either side are plateaus; highlands rise to the south of the lake. Malawi is a thin country extending down the western edge of the lake and thrusting deeply southward into the interior of Mozambique.

Because of its size and terrain, Malawi is not as well known for its animal life as other African countries. It maintains its share of wildlife parks and preserves, however. These include Kasungu National Park, home of cape buffalo, large hoofed beasts, and predators. Monkeys swing through Malawi's forests; antelopes dart through the meadows and hills.

David Livingstone gave Lake Nyasa and Nyasaland their names (*nyasa* means "lake" in an African dialect of the region) when he first set eyes on them in the late 1850s. Soon, interested by Livingstone's reports from the region, Scottish churches began sending other missionaries to Nyasaland. By the time the colonial era began in the 1890s, several Christian denominations had established mission outposts, including the Roman Catholics.

Before the colonial era, countless people of the region were captured and enslaved at the hands of raiding Africans and of Arab and Portuguese traders based in Mozambique. Slave taking was one aspect of Africa that incensed Livingstone—who otherwise loved the continent and its people and patiently learned all he could about them. Slave trading continued into the nineteenth century, when England ultimately led the way to ending it on an international level.

It's curious that the British government in the late 1700s felt compelled to go to the aid of Africans in distress . . . and a century later would impose a colonial system that placed Africans under the thumbs of white *imperialists*. Colonialism, while hardly the equivalent of slavery, was structured to benefit visiting white companies and colonists at the expense of Africans who had occupied the land for ages. Although European leaders told the world (and themselves) that they were establishing colonial governments for the good of the Africans, they immediately made it clear they were in the continent for their own interests. Yet, most nineteenth-century voices of protest against slavery became silent when it came to the issue of colonial policy.

Their silence persisted well into the next century. "During the 1920s," wrote historian John D. Hargreaves, "those citizens of western Europe who were aware that their governments controlled substantial territories and populations in tropical Africa usually assumed this to be a fact of nature, or at least of history."

What happened in Nyasaland was a classic example of how the colonial system worked. English farmers settled in the colony on the best lands. To raise revenue for its own operation, the colonial government taxed the Africans. In order to make money to pay their taxes, the Africans had to go to work for the occupying whites, either on the farms or in company mines across the southern part of the continent. The wages the laborers received were appalling, as was the segregated treatment. Thus, while the Africans endured virtually enforced labor at meager pay with no way to improve their lot in life (and in their own country, at that), the British extracted very cheap labor to work their lucrative new enterprises—and made others pay much of the expense of colonial government. In modern business jargon, it was a "win-win" situation from the British viewpoint . . . "lose-lose" from the African perspective. Other colonial territories witnessed variations of the process, but the fundamental approach generally was the same.

Malawi is approximately the size of Pennsylvania. Like other countries in the subtropics, it annually has a dry, cool season (May–October) and a wet, hot season (November–April). During the wet months it rains almost every day. Its vegetation ranges from grassy savannahs to bamboo and papyrus swamps. Forested areas exhibit interesting trees such as the flowering acacia.

Victoria Falls, 1911 *Victoria Falls is a spectacular waterfall located about midway along the course of the Zambezi River at the border between Zambia and Zimbabwe. It is about twice as wide and twice as deep as Niagara Falls. David Livingstone was the first European to see the falls (1855). He named it for England's Queen Victoria. Today tourists from all parts of the world visit Victoria Falls and the surrounding national parks of Zambia and Zimbabwe. In 1989 the falls was designated a World Heritage site by UNESCO.*

ZAMBIA: THE REGION'S NORTHERNMOST COUNTRY

In British colonial times, today's Zambia was Northern Rhodesia. Before the Europeans came, it was in many ways like other parts of Africa. Its ancient history is one of wandering peoples and village communities.

Constructing the Victoria Falls Bridge, c. 1910 *The Victoria Falls Bridge over the Zambezi River carries rail, automobile, and pedestrian traffic between Zambia and Zimbabwe. It is one of four major crossings of the river.*

The bridge, which is 650 feet long and 300 feet above the river, was designed by Sir Ralph Freeman, (1880–1950) and constructed between 1905 and 1911.

Zambia is a landlocked *plateau* country cut by steep river gorges, about the size of the Spanish/Portuguese peninsula. Several impressive lakes lie on its borders and in its interior, including natural Lake Tanganyika in the north and man-made

Lake Kariba in the south. The River Congo—Africa's second longest, after the Nile—originates in northern Zambia, where it is called the Chapezi, and flows generally westward through south-central Africa into the Atlantic Ocean. But it's the Zambezi for which the country is best known and from which it gets its name. The Zambezi and Congo are but two of many rivers that carve the country into a fascinating natural landscape.

Zambia is noted for its mining industries, notably copper, zinc, and lead. Its main cities were built during the twentieth century, some of them originating as mining camps. The buildings and thoroughfares of the country today are western-style.

Throughout the modernization of its mining industry and its partial "Europeanization" under colonial rule, Zambia has remained rich in wildlife and natural wonders. It has thick, hilly forests. In the open savannahs, peculiar *baobab* trees here and there stand starkly against the sky; they are known to locals as "upside down" trees because their limbs splay outward at the top, resembling a root system. Giant anthills in some places are as large as huts. Thousands of species of animals and birds, some of which are found only in Zambia, can be seen. Lake Tanganyika contains hundreds of fish species, including 200-pound catfish and Goliath tiger fish.

Famous Victoria Falls (*Mosi Oa Tunya*, or "Smoke That Thunders," to Zambians and Zimbabweans), more than a mile wide and 355 feet deep, on the River Zambezi is one of the planet's most spectacular sights. Mail trains in colonial days would stop on the Zambezi bridge to let passengers view the falls. In high-water seasons, the roar of the falls can be heard miles away.

The Zambezi is a time-honored river. Louis Livingston Seaman, a visitor to the region who already had witnessed many of the world's most dazzling waterfalls and waterways, wrote in 1911 that "while the Zambesi lacks many of the individual features which make these great natural attractions unique in their beauty, it nevertheless possesses, in its exquisite setting

Stone Ruins, Great Zimbabwe, c. 1911 *Great Zimbabwe was a thriving empire from A.D. 1100 to 1500. It lies in southeastern Zimbabwe, some 17 miles southeast of Masvingo (formerly Fort Victoria). This photograph is of the Acropolis ruins. Believed to have been the spiritual and religious center of the city, the Acropolis is perched on a steep hill. At some points the walls are twenty feet thick. It is the oldest part of Greater Zimbabwe. Archaeological evidence shows that the first stones were laid there about A.D. 900.*

of emerald and tropic luxuriance, its grottos and rain forests, its dancing cascades and raging cataracts, its roseate sprays and frolicking rainbows, a diversity of charms surpassing them all."

As for the falls, Seaman wrote that "even the Inferno of Dante, in the passage over the Styx, as pictured by Doré, does not surpass this as a spectacle of terrifying beauty." He elaborated: "From immemorial times an atmosphere of mystery and superstition has hung over the Falls, so profound that Livingstone, who discovered them in 1855, had the greatest difficulty in persuading his followers to accompany him, as they believed the region to be the home of monsters and devils of destruction. Vestiges of these traditions still exist, although the Cape to Cairo Railroad, which crosses the river less than half a mile below the Falls, is rapidly dispelling them."

Livingstone himself described the huge waterfall with a tinge of trauma:

> I believe that no one could perceive where the vast body of water went: it seemed to lose itself in the earth, the opposite lip of the fissure into which it disappeared being only 80 feet distant. At least, I did not comprehend it until, creeping with awe to the verge, I peered down into a large rent which had been made from bank to bank of the broad Zambesi and saw that a stream of a thousand yards broad leaped down a hundred feet and then became suddenly compressed into a space of 15 or 20 yards . . .

Many other waterfalls attract tourists from other countries. Some Zambians believe these falls house their ancestors' spirits. Although conditions are hot and humid in the river gorges during summer, Zambia is known worldwide for its pleasant climate.

Zambia is home to a diversity of people and lifestyles. Some live in modern cities; others live in remote villages little different from those of their ancestors.

ZIMBABWE: AN OLD KINGDOM YIELDS TO THE PASSAGE OF TIME

Zimbabwe, another landlocked nation, lies south of Zambia between the Zambezi and Limpopo rivers. It is roughly the size of California. Along its northern border with Zambia is Lake Kariba, which provides hydroelectric power for both countries.

The areas near the two rivers are lowlands. Across the country rises a fertile plateau region known as the "high veld." It has excellent grazing for livestock. The landscape is unique for its natural outcrops of stone, called *kopjes*.

It was in the highlands that "Great Zimbabwe," a prominent city-state, existed during the fourteenth and fifteenth centuries. Its people were traders who established one of the greatest cities in precolonial Africa. They conducted brisk commerce with East African seaports of old, whose merchants in turn were trading with mariners from India, Arabia, and probably China. Great Zimbabwe's most important trade item was gold. The Shona population, modern Zimbabwe's majority ethnic group, descend from the people of Great Zimbabwe.

The ruins of Great Zimbabwe's massive, curved stone walls and buildings can be seen today in southern Zimbabwe. (One translation of "Zimbabwe" is "structures in stone.") At places, the ancient city's outer wall is more than thirty feet high and seventeen feet thick. Great Zimbabwe clearly was a wealthy city with wide-ranging connections. Archaeologists have discovered ornate artifacts, objects of gold, items apparently acquired through trade with the Orient, and impressive stone sculpture. These relics tell of a fascinating and highly prosperous civilization. Eventually, though, it weakened as other trading centers grew in southern Africa.

The Shona people who have kept their ancestral religions hold rituals in honor of their forebears. They believe their ancestors watch over them. If the living show respect, their ancestral spirits will protect them; if not, their dead relatives can bring harm.

The ferocious, sweeping Zulu campaigns of the first half of the nineteenth century affected not just South Africa, the Zulus' homeland, but neighboring regions including Zimbabwe and other parts of Southeast Africa. Although the infamous Zulu hordes themselves—thousands of warriors strong—ranged mostly to the south, some of the African peoples they defeated fled northward. They in turn displaced inhabitants of the borderlands and beyond, as far north as modern-day Malawi.

MOZAMBIQUE ON THE COAST

Mozambique is Southeast Africa's coastal country, with more than 1,500 miles of shoreline. The land is fairly flat and grassy near the Indian Ocean coast, rising to highlands and mountains near the Zimbabwe border.

Some sixty rivers flow to the sea through the nation's lowlands. Some are fairly narrow and short. Most notable is the Zambezi, which, as we've seen, originates in the heart of southern Africa and passes through the center of Mozambique. Other large rivers include the Limpopo and Lurio. An interesting thing about Mozambique's rivers, especially the smaller waterways, is how radically they change during the region's wet and dry seasons. From June to August, there is little rainfall and therefore little water running into the rivers. Certain watercourses literally dry up. They fill quickly when the rainy season begins, however.

Mozambique has two freshwater reservoirs in the north: Lake Malawi, which forms much of its border with the nation of Malawi, and the Cabora Bassa Reservoir, a man-made lake on the Zambezi.

"Bush" people—groups of wandering hunter-gatherers—are believed to have been Mozambique's earliest humans. Around the fourth century A.D., farming and trading peoples from the west and north began settling in the bush country. One group, the Maravi, developed a thriving trade with Arabs who were navigating down the east coast of Africa. Sofala became one of the busiest ports in the region. The Maravi brought ivory, slaves, gold, palm oil, and other items from the interior. In exchange, the Arabs gave them such goods as cloth, ceramics, and salt.

Water Holes, Barotseland, c. 1903–1905 *This photograph was taken in Barotseland, one of the few traditional kingdoms recognized by Great Britain within what was then Rhodesia. From 1876 to 1916, Lewanika ruled Barotseland. Fearful of the Portuguese as well as other native chiefs, Lewanika brought Barotseland under British protection in exchange for mineral concessions. Despite Lewanika's "protected" status, the British whittled away at his authority. In 1906 the British insisted on the abolition of slavery and serfdom. Gradually, Barotseland became tied to South Africa politically and economically.*

Portuguese mariners arrived at the Mozambique coast at the end of the fifteenth century. They quickly took an interest, and a domineering role, that would last almost 500 years. Armed with firearms and cannons, the Portuguese easily took the best trading sites from Arab merchants; they allowed the Arabs to remain but demanded tribute. They secured the trading port at Sofala in 1505. Then, following the course of the great River Zambezi, they set about to establish outposts into the Southeast African mainland. Meanwhile, they built stone forts and set up trading operations all the way up the coast to the "horn" of the continent (present-day Somalia).

In the coming years, Portuguese forces marched inland, conquering ancient peoples, looking for gold, and opening some of the land for Portuguese farmers to settle. But they never made solid, lasting progress in Mozambique. One reason was that Portuguese landholders, called *prazeiros*, were not very loyal to the Lisbon government; they looked after their own interests instead. If their estates proved unprofitable or the country and climate too harsh, the owners simply abandoned them.

While many European traders in Africa earned unsavory reputations for their use of force, the Portuguese were particularly cruel. They destroyed the villages of African and Arab leaders who resisted them. And by controlling the coastal ports, they became key players in the vilest of history's commercial endeavors: the human slave trade.

African kingdoms had enslaved captives during their ongoing warfare for centuries before the Europeans arrived. But the coming of the white traders created a new, vast, distant market. Soon raiders were attacking rural villages in both the interior and coastal areas and carrying off able-bodied men and women. Tied together, often forced to carry ivory tusks and other heavy trade items, the prisoners were marched—often for days and weeks—to slave trading posts. Many died on the trail, or were left to die if they became too weak to walk.

By the end of the eighteenth century, at the height of the African slave trade, an estimated 9,000 slaves annually were being shipped from Mozambique ports. Most were transported around the Cape of Good Hope and carried to the Americas to work on plantations. Many were taken to Portugal's South American colony of Brazil. The slave trade from Mozambique did not abate until 1844, when British naval vessels offshore began to crack down on slave ships.

When the great colonial parceling of Africa by the European powers began in the late 1800s, the Portuguese, clinging to their Zambezi trading towns, were able to "claim" Mozambique. But they would never gain firm control over their colony.

The Island Nation

Madagascar is linked closely to Africa in terms of both distance and recent history. Yet, it is almost a separate world. Much of its plant and animal life, developing over a period of centuries, is found only on this strange island. And while inhabitants of the modern-day Southeast African mainland descend mostly from the Bantu migration from northern and central Africa, Madagascar is thought to have been settled by Indonesians—people from the Orient, some 4,000 miles away. They are thought to have arrived about 2,000 years ago. Archaeologists have found no human remains to suggest earlier civilizations on the island—although it should be noted that much of Madagascar is remote and remains largely unexplored.

In more recent centuries, black Africans arrived on Madagascar, most of them as slaves brought by traders. Through intermarriage, this Indonesian-African mixture has become the Malagasy people. Their common language contains subtle elements of Arabic. This feature, coupled with centuries-old ruins, suggests the island was a trading center well known to mariners from Muslim lands.

Charles F. Swingle, an American scientist who visited the island in the 1920s, described the Malagasy as "handsome, straight-haired, brown-skinned people of mysterious origin . . . How they managed to transport themselves for thousands of miles, across the Indian Ocean, to their present isolated homeland is an interesting puzzle. Equally interesting is the fact that, although Madagascar lies only 240 miles off the east coast of Africa, the natives show little mixture with African blood."

Some 8,000 plant varieties are found on the island. Most of them live in the eastern rain forest. Notable among them are the island's many varieties of orchids. Madagascar also is known for strange tree species, including the bulb-trunked *baobab* ("bottle tree," as some westerners called it) and the fan-limbed *ravinala*, or "traveler's palm." *Ravinala* leaves naturally collect water condensation and are so broad that some of the Malagasy people traditionally have used them as plates for rice meals.

Madagascar's most famous creature is the lemur, a long-tailed, monkey-faced, tree-hopping animal indigenous only to Madagascar and the nearby Comoro Islands. Madagascar also is home to an estimated half the world's chameleon species. Offshore, humpback whales breach the surface of the Indian Ocean.

From a mountainous plateau at its center, Madagascar descends down to the sea. Its terrain varies from dry desert in the south to tropical forests and fertile farmland in the north. The country is cut through by many short rivers, some of them breaking into lovely waterfalls. Volcanic islands lie off the northwestern coast. Coral reefs protect much of the island's shoreline.

Rains regularly sweep in from the ocean to the east, bringing the northern sections of Madagascar an annual average rainfall of more than 100 inches a year. From December to March, it is likely to be struck by an Indian Ocean cyclone. In 2000, a seasonal storm killed 150 islanders and ruined thousands of acres of rice fields. Cholera, a dreaded plague that has threatened different parts of the world for centuries, was spread by cyclone-caused flooding.

WHAT ATTRACTED THE EUROPEANS?

Obviously, Southeast Africa is a region of great beauty and natural resources. Two major fields of interest lured foreigners.

The first, as we've seen, was commerce. Traders from Arabia for centuries had been sailing down Africa's east coast, soon to be followed by traders from Europe sailing around the Cape of Good Hope.

The second incentive was the spread of the Gospel. The traditional religious beliefs of Southeast Africans were to be joined by two major foreign faiths. Islam already had arrived by the time the first Europeans did, having been brought to the region by Arab traders. Islam became well established in the coastal areas and by the beginning of the colonial era was spreading to the interior. About the same period, Protestant missionaries from the British Isles were beginning to explore southern Africa. Most notable among them, as we'll see in the next chapter, was Scotsman David Livingstone. Roman Catholic missionaries were active in the region during the late 1800s, as were Dutch Protestants.

60.B.

Zambian, 1901 *This ferryman took the Scottish missionary-explorer David Livingstone across the Lulimala River in his dying days. Livingstone was on an expedition to find the source of the Nile, but succumbed to dysentery on May 1, 1873; his heart was buried in Africa, but his body was carried to Zanzibar and shipped back to Great Britain for burial.*

2

TRADERS, TYCOONS, AND MISSIONARIES

The two early objectives of the Europeans—trade and the establishment of Christian missions—sometimes conflicted. Tragically, as we noted earlier, much of the trading quickly focused on two particularly valuable items: ivory and human slaves. The importance of the devastation caused by the animal trade—vast herds of big game decimated for their tusks—would not be understood fully until the late twentieth century. But the enforced labor, torture, and *deportation* of humans immediately was apparent to European societies. Not just individuals but sometimes entire families and villages were taken captive and marched to coastal trading posts, forced to carry heavy cargo as they trudged, bound, through the wilds. A few protests were hurled, but most sympathizers in Europe, deciding there was little they could do to prevent these outrages in a distant land, kept quiet and tried not to think of them.

Christian *abolitionists*, though, launched a concerted effort to halt slave trading. After years of mounting pressure, the British government outlawed slavery in the early 1800s. Furthermore, it began posting warships off the African coast to intercept slave vessels and punish the commanders.

Many of the missionaries sent to Africa were ardent abolitionists. The most famous one in the southern realm of the continent was Scotsman David Livingstone.

Influenced by famous antislavery advocate William Wilber-
force, Livingstone was a doctor who began his work in Africa
in 1840.

Unlike most Europeans who would follow him to the continent, Livingstone was one white man who dedicated himself to
Africa. He did not enter the unknown interior in quest of riches
or land. He sought to save souls, to provide medical help to the
people he found, and simply to explore places never before visited by those of his own race. Almost immediately after arriv-
ing in South Africa in 1841, he began to learn some of the
native languages and to study the customs of the people. He
expected to face many challenges—although he may have been
given more than he anticipated.

Two years into his career he ran afoul of a wounded lion. The
beast seized his left shoulder in its jaws. "Growling horribly,"
he later recounted, "he shook me as a terrier dog shakes a rat. It
caused a sort of dreaminess in which there was no sense of pain
or feeling of terror, although I was conscious of all that happened." Thankfully, a skillful spearman was able to kill the lion,
but the injury left Livingstone with a lingering pain for the
remainder of his life.

A few years later, Livingstone ventured with his wife and
three young children across a desert hundreds of miles farther
into the interior. He was looking for a new mission site. With
their water depleted, the entire family almost perished before
the journey's end. Later in his travels, he would endure fevers,
near starvation, food poisoning, and other afflictions. Tropical
sickness ultimately took his life in 1873.

Livingstone's explorations led him thousands of miles
through much of lower Africa over a period of more than thirty
years. Among other discoveries, he was the first white man to
see the great falls on the Zambezi which he named after Queen
Victoria. But he was much more than an explorer. Livingstone
became a forceful activist against the slave trade that ravaged
many of the African villages and kingdoms. In his later life, his
white colleagues sometimes found him demanding and difficult

to get along with. Africans, on the other hand, found him patient and kind.

Other missionaries who worked in the region during the late 1800s included François Coillard and Henri Dupont.

THE EUROPEANS "SCRAMBLE" TO CONTROL AFRICA

By the 1880s the European powers were taking an interest in Africa for reasons other than winning Christian converts and exploring mysterious geography. Trade had become important, and different countries had established bases around the coast. Using African middlemen, they were bringing valuable goods out of the interior, notably minerals and animal skins and tusks.

Otto von Bismarck, chancellor of Prussia (Germany), summoned representatives from the other European nations to Berlin in autumn 1884. He wished to discuss a sensible approach to the African question. On the surface, his expressed desire was to "help" the Africans—to bring peace to warring peoples and prosperity by means of modern industry. Other leaders agreed, but what they really wanted, as history proved, was to make sure of their own national interests. If there were gains to be made by exerting control in strategic parts of the southern continent, they wanted to have a presence there. In Africa, they not only could obtain desirable commodities; they also could trade and sell some of the products their own factories were producing.

The Berlin West Africa Conference resulted in a formal document. None of the nations were bold enough to make territorial claims. (Those would come soon enough.) For the moment, they voiced concern over the "moral and material well-being" of the African people. In the process, they established rules for involving themselves in Africa's affairs. If a foreign nation was interested in a specific part of Africa, the representatives agreed, it must do two things. First, it must declare its intentions openly. Second, it must actually establish some form of authority in the area. A long history of trading in a territory was not enough; the western country must have a military force, government agency or representative agency in the area. Thus began what many historians consider to be the "carving up" of Africa. The colonial era was about to begin.

THE BRITISH REACH NORTHWARD

Minerals were the main attraction of British interests in what soon would become Rhodesia. "Mining! That is the magic word in this land," wrote W. Robert Moore, an American, well into the colonial era. "Broken Hill, 300 air miles north of Livingstone, lives . . . for its mines of lead, zinc, and vanadium. Northward still are Ndola, Mufuliru, Nkana, Kitwe, and a number of other strange place names—strange, that is, except to copper miners. In this region, and stretching over into the Belgian Congo, lies a vast copper belt. It covers an area some 75 miles long and 20 miles across. Here are some of the biggest copper mines in the world."

It didn't take long for the British to discover the area's mineral treasures. Oxford-educated Cecil Rhodes was an English businessman who decided as a young man to move to South Africa. In poor health, he hoped the climate would be good for him. Not only was the climate pleasant; his business fortune soon flourished. He made his money in diamonds around Kimberley.

Rhodes formed the British South Africa Company in the 1880s and in time was named prime minister of England's Cape Colony. A champion of English imperialism, he wanted to expand British control northward across the River Limpopo in what is now Zimbabwe. He once stated: "If there is a God, I think that what he would like me to do is to paint as much of Africa British-red as possible."

Rhodes believed there was much mineral wealth to be had there. He wanted to block the German government and the Boer (Dutch) settlers from expanding their holdings in the Transvaal region located south of the Limpopo, and the Portuguese from infringing from Mozambique. Rhodes despised the Portuguese, labeling them "a curse to any place they have occupied."

In the long run, Rhodes hoped to contribute to a vital road and rail system that would extend the whole length of Africa, from British-controlled Capetown at the southern tip to British-controlled Cairo near the Mediterranean coast on the River Nile, some 3,000 miles north. This line (which never was connected) naturally would have to pass through Zimbabwe and into the East African lake region, source of the Nile.

The British government liked Rhodes's ideas. It was Lord Salisbury, England's famous foreign secretary and prime minister, who conceived of the "Cape-to-Cairo" plan with Harry Johnston, the British vice-consul to Mozambique. Such a transportation line would make England the supreme European power in all Africa. Salisbury had another reason for taking an interest in Rhodes's scheme: Rhodes was rich. If the government would charter his company and let him carry out his operation in Southeast Africa, he basically could fund it himself. Rhodes later would refer to the Cape-to-Cairo fantasy as "my hobby."

Much of lower Zimbabwe was a native warrior state, Matabeleland, ruled by the powerful Ndebele people. To the east was Mashonaland, home of the weaker Shona group. In the mid 1880s, one of Rhodes's agents, Charles Rudd, obtained mineral rights from the Matabele chief, Lobengula. In June 1890 a force of more than 200 settlers accompanied by hundreds of soldiers invaded Mashonaland.

This was the famous "Pioneer Column." The hardy settlers were lured by Rhodes's impressive offer of rewards: 3,000 acres of land per man plus gold-digging rights. Making their way slowly through the savannah, they built military outposts and settlements. In just three months, they "settled" Mashonaland—as well, that is, as such a small number of people could be expected to claim such a large territory. They soon were joined by other settlers eager to have their own vast farmlands, regardless of the remoteness.

Naturally, this angered Lobengula, who considered Mashonaland part of his domain. It also angered the Portuguese in the east, who had assumed trading privileges among the Shona in Mashonaland for two centuries. Neither, though, was powerful enough to prevent Rhodes from making Mashonaland a British territory.

Rhodes was disappointed to find little gold. His settlers eagerly built cattle farms, however. Soon they were claiming land in neighboring Matabeleland and feuding with native cattle herders. Ndebele warriors prepared for a fight.

Neither Chief Lobengula nor Rhodes wanted war. Lobengula sent representatives to discuss the crisis with British officials at Cape Town, but they were ambushed and slaughtered along the road. "I thought you came to dig gold," Lobengula said of Rhodes, "but it seems that you have come to rob me of my people and country as well."

The first Matabele War in 1893 was a disaster for Lobengula and his people. With repeating Maxim guns, the whites defeated the proud Ndebele—who were ravaged by a smallpox epidemic. In one battle, almost a thousand warriors were cut down, compared to just four fatalities on the British side. After the whites occupied the Ndebele capital of Bulawayo, Lobengula, in flight, tried to surrender. He sent a note to the British commander with a bag of gold. "Take this and go back," the chief pleaded. "I am conquered." But the offer never reached the authorities; treacherous European messengers stole the money and didn't deliver Lobengula's note.

With British pursuers drawing close, Lobengula poisoned himself. The victorious Rhodes had practically doubled the size of his colony. The victors put the Ndebele men to work on their farms and abused the women. They seized Ndebele cattle as prizes of war.

Natural calamities made things even worse for the defeated Africans. The Ndebele and Shona were plagued by drought, locusts, and an outbreak of *rinderpest* that killed many of their livestock. Things got so bad that in 1896, these two peoples—

Bemba Coiffure, c. 1896 *British explorer Poulett Weatherley was inspired by David Livingstone. In the 1890s, Weatherley explored Lake Mweru, paralleling Livingstone's route in central Africa. In 1896, because of Weatherley's fearless hunting skills, this Bemba chief befriended him. The chief's influence extended from Lake Tanganyika to Lake Mweru.*

Kisi Island, c. 1896 *Poulett Weatherley was the first European to circumvent Lake Bangweulu in north-eastern Zambia. There are three islands within the lake, which is approximately forty-five miles long and twenty-four miles wide. Today the three islands are uninhabited, but there were thriving villages on these islands when Weatherley became the first European to visit them more than 100 years ago. Weatherley wrote that his arrival on Kisi was "a perfect picture." The people greeted him on their knees, clapping their hands. "[It was] a peaceful and prosperous sight," he wrote, and continued as follows:*

In front of the village, which nestled amid a mass of lipupu and banana trees for almost 100 yards back from the beach, there was a long stretch of beautiful fresh grass—almost turf. On this many sheep and goats were browsing, tended by little mites in the barb of nature. All round, at the back of the village, were fields of grain and cassava, and about 500 yards to the left there was an enormous clump of trees called m'situ. Beyond this again was the hill on which I intended to form my camp. There were many small canoes drawn up on the sand, and numerous fishing-nets . . . .

The morning after my arrival, there was as an enormous gathering of natives at my camp, all squatted in semicircles round their headmen, and the whole in a circle round my camp. The women kept outside the male crowd, and chiefly came to do the bartering part of the business. The chief of the island was a very good sort, and took the most intelligent interest in my guns. His great joy was the "breaking" and "mending" of my rifles. People used to come and beg me to "break" my guns, so that they might see them "mended." Goodness only knows how far many traveled, or how many came, just to see this extraordinary bit of "medicine."

Kisi Island, c. 1896 *Weatherley continued his narrative:*

I walked across Kisi to the west coast to take the sun. . . . I was walking along, buried in thought, when I heard a soft clapping of hands to my left. Looking in that direction, I saw a comely middle-aged matron totaing and smiling amidst her cassava. Her coiffure was coloured red with ukula and oil, and bright with beads. She wore many bright iron bangles as ornaments, and was clothed in mitai (bark) cloth dyed with ukula, and neatly embroidered with patterns sewn with light-coloured grass, which in the sunshine shone like gold thread. He neck was encircled by two or three rows of beads, amongst which I recognized some I had introduced on the island. She had risen from her knees, and was regarding me with great curiosity, and I trust, admiration, when I turned my face to her and, smiling, said, "Good morning mother." The buxom dame's face simply beamed. Down she flopped on her exceedingly well-covered knees, and announced, her face rippling over with smiles, "I am the wife of Chamata." I cannot say that the information interested me particularly, but I could not help congratulating Chamata, whoever he may have been, on the possession of a lady so evidently proud of being his spouse (Royal Geographical Society, *Journal,* 1898, pp. 252–253).

recent opponents—joined in a rebellion against the European settlers. But they were poorly organized. While some native forces aggressively attacked the whites, others refused to cooperate and some gave supplies to the enemy.

Although unprepared for the uprising initially, the British gradually destroyed the Shona rebels. Then they turned their attention to the west and, in 1897, forced the Ndebele to surrender. Rhodes and the British had claimed their interior colony. They also had planted seeds of anger that would live for generations and eventually would grow into an irrepressible demand for native rule.

Devastated by their unsuccessful rebellion of 1896–1897, the Shona people in Southern Rhodesia turned to Christianity in great numbers. The missionaries provided a form of refuge, and in time the church would become an important influence in the drive toward independence. Many twentieth-century nationalist leaders across Africa were educated at mission schools, especially in southern Africa. In 1884—even before the famous Berlin Conference convened to discuss the pending European colonization of Africa, a political newspaper called *Imvo Zabantsundu* ("Native Opinion") was founded in the Cape Colony. And when blacks began severing ties with white-run missions and forming native Christian congregations—also as early as the 1880s—their churches became platforms for bringing together peoples of different tribes.

Beyond the Zambezi, with the help of missionaries, the British South Africa Company obtained treaties with two important area kingdoms: the Lozi on the upper Zambezi and the Bemba farther north. When other rulers refused to cooperate, Rhodes used force. By the mid 1890s, the company's northern domain—haughtily named Rhodesia after the organization's founder—had been forged as a *charter colony* (*i.e.,* one administered by a chartered company rather than a crown colony overseen directly by the British government). After the 1896 uprising, the land was split into two colonies: Northern Rhodesia and Southern Rhodesia. They would become, respectively, the modern nations of Zambia and Zimbabwe.

The British established the town of Livingstone at the Victoria Falls as the capital of Northern Rhodesia. It became a major center on the rail line that connected South Africa with Britain's territories to the north. Lusaka, the modern capital of Zambia, in early colonial years was just a railroad siding, by contrast. It was named after a famous chief known for his feats in hunting the elephant. During the British presence it steadily grew and was made capital of Northern Rhodesia in 1932.

In 1923 Southern Rhodesia's whites voted to become a crown colony. Although officially under British rule, they essentially began to govern themselves. Salisbury became the capital of Southern Rhodesia. Northern Rhodesia, meanwhile, became a British "protectorate" with an administration strongly influenced from London. Compared to the south, it had a much smaller white population clamoring to control their own destinies.

English colonials weren't averse to taking advantage of the native inhabitants. Through the tax system and rules the colonials imposed, they literally forced Africans to work their mines. Melville Chater, reporting from "The Pioneer Colony" of Rhodesia for *The National Geographic Magazine* in the mid 1930s, commented on the daunting task of "administering" a work camp of 6,000 African coal miners housed in huts. "This is effected through a Government-controlled régime of native reserves, tribal chiefs, and a modified adherence to the tribes' communal and patriarchal system."

To the Africans, of course, the arrangement was lamentable. Some Europeans found it lamentable, too, but for different reasons. From the first, they decried the uncomfortable conditions in Africa. Consul Harry Johnston wrote huffily to Cecil Rhodes in 1893,

I have spared neither the risk of my own life, the abandonment of comfort, nor the right to rest at times like other people. Sundays and weekdays, mornings and evenings I am to be found either slaving at my desk, or tearing about the country on horseback, or trudging twenty miles a day on foot or sweltering in boats or being horribly sea-sick in

Southern Africa about 1890

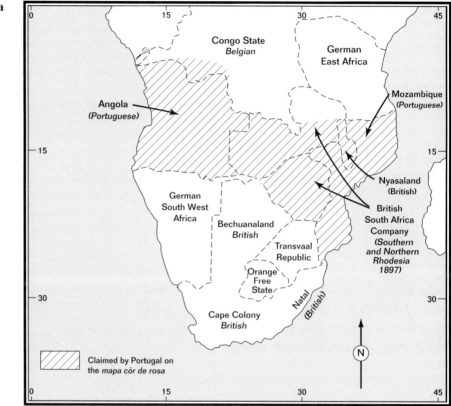

Lake Nyasa steamers. I have to carry on in my office, myself, a most onerous correspondence in Swahili, which I have to write in the Arabic character, in Portuguese, in French, and in English. I have had to acquire a certain mastery over Hindustani to deal with the Indian troops. I have learnt three native languages besides Swahili in order to talk straight to the people. I have undertaken grave responsibilities, and I have devoted myself to the most wearisome and niggling tasks. One day I am working out a survey which has to be of scrupulous accuracy, and another day I am doing what a few years ago I never thought I should be called upon to do—undertaking the whole responsibility of directing military operations. I

Hunter with Gun, c. 1896 *This hunter was photographed by Poulett Weatherley at the southern end of Lake Mweru, a lake in central Africa bordered to the east by Zambia and to the west by the Congo.*

Hunter with Bow and Arrow, c. 1896 *This hunter, using the traditional bow and arrow, also was photographed in the Lake Mweru area.*

Mweru Native, c. 1896 *Weatherley photographed this native living on the shore of Lake Mweru. The young man probably was posed with the British rifle. Note his coiffure.*

Poulett Weatherley, c. 1896 *This is a photograph of Poulett Weatherley, his boat* Vigilant, *and his crew after their circumnavigation of Lake Bangweulu. In 1898 the Royal Geographical Society honored Weatherley for his three years of explorations in central Africa.*

have even had myself taught to fire Maxim guns and seven-pounder cannon, I, who detest loud noises and have a horror of explosives.

Soon after conquering the territory, the whites set about to establish a viable transportation system. By 1935 the two Rhodesias were crossed by some 2,000 miles of railroads. These, combined with dirt highways, were vital for linking the colonies' mineral- and food-producing centers to the outside world. The British also established telegraph and telephone lines in the 1890s that still would be in use a century later in rural regions.

EUROPEAN FOOTHOLDS AROUND
THE LAKE SHORE

It was during the early 1880s that Scottish missionaries and business interests combined forces around the "lakes" region of eastern and southeastern Africa. Their African Lakes Company, they hoped, would end slave trading in the region once and for all. They influenced the government in London to create a British consulate for Mozambique and Nyasaland and to dispatch army attacks against slaving operations in the area.

Obviously, the missionaries wanted to combat slavery for moral reasons. Did their business associates share those concerns? More likely, the commercial enterprises recognized that by depleting the supply of able-bodied Africans in the interior, the slave kings were weakening a potentially strong market for purchasing/trading European goods. At the same time, the raiders were removing thousands of strong workers—people who could provide very cheap labor for white farmers who were moving into the countryside.

Many historians agree the missionaries had noble objectives in colonial Africa but became partners, probably unavoidably, with other Europeans whose objectives were far from noble. Jomo Kenyatta, Kenya's first president after independence, once explained the dilemma famously in a nutshell: "When the missionaries came, the Africans had the land and the Christians had the Bible. They taught us to pray with our eyes closed. When we opened them they had the land and we had the Bible."

In Malawi, Great Britain created the British Central Africa Protectorate in 1893. In 1907 it officially was called Nyasaland, its name until the country became independent in 1964. The British began building a system of roads and rail lines into the region—not for the benefit of the Africans who lived there, but for the white settlers. By developing careful alliances with strategically important chiefs, England established a fairly secure colonial arrangement that would last some seventy years.

"As for Nyasaland," noted historian Robin Hallett, "the territory was regarded by many Europeans in the 1920s and 1930s as a model colony, a country untroubled by politics. The *bwanas*, the 'great white chiefs' of the colonial administration, 'ruled it,' according to one of their European contemporaries, 'with a fairness, tolerance, and incorruptibility that was the envy of other dependencies.'"

THE PORTUGUESE MANEUVER TO SURVIVE

In Mozambique, Portugal held some semblance of control in the late 1800s. Whether it truly *exerted* control was a different matter. In the words of Hallett, "Empires are built with money and guns and blood and sweat, not with paper treatises, historical memories, and political rhetoric." Portugal was not a particularly powerful player in the international politics of the late nineteenth century. Truth be known, it was a relatively poor, unstable western nation. Even into the 1960s the per capita income of Portuguese citizens was substantially less than that of South African citizens. Members of Portugal's governing class protested the morality—and cost—of maintaining overseas colonies.

Nevertheless, Great Britain seemed willing to let Portugal have the southeastern coast and focus its own attention on Rhodes's thrust into the south-central part of the continent. England and Portugal in 1891 signed a treaty letting Portugal remain in control of the region in which it had been trading for centuries.

With England and Germany muscling in on territories around Mozambique, Portugal preserved its holdings largely by chartering commercial land companies to control economic development and related affairs. British investors in time bought the lion's share of stock in the major land companies. That did not seriously undermine Portuguese influence, however, for the companies met with scant success. They earned little in return for their investments. The Nyasa Company dissolved in 1929, the Mozambique Company in 1942.

Certain native tribes from the early years of the colonial era had determined to oust the Europeans. Guerrilla groups began raiding Portuguese targets in 1894. Various tribes along the River Zambezi and elsewhere continued to resist for almost twenty years. They were put down one by one. But it was a costly undertaking, and Portugal never was able to exert control very far beyond its river and coastal trading centers.

Mozambique was not a land of opportunity for native Africans. If they worked for the Europeans, they were paid little. The Portuguese controlled agriculture, dictating where crops could and couldn't be sold. A "hut tax" effectively forced Africans to work for the Portuguese at meager pay, much of which had to be paid to the government.

With little job incentive at home, thousands of blacks from Mozambique went to work in the British-run mines of neighboring South Africa and Rhodesia. The Portuguese administration turned this labor pattern to its advantage by charging the mining companies a portion of the migrant workers' earnings—a form of labor tax.

For much of the colonial period, Portugal was unable to entice many people from the home country to relocate to Mozambique. Thousands of Portuguese in the early twentieth century emigrated across the Atlantic to Brazil, while comparatively few opted for Southeast Africa. After World War II, from 1945 to the early 1970s, the government created new incentives. By the mid 1970s almost a quarter of a million whites (still a small minority) lived in Mozambique. Many were small-scale farmers and shop owners.

Slow Progress Colonizing the Island

Madagascar began appearing on European maps around 1500. Portuguese explorer Diego Dias landed on the island that year, and during the next few centuries, Portugal used Madagascar as an important supply stop for its seafarers who made long trading voyages around Africa to the Orient.

In the 1600s British trading vessels also began using the island. The English tried to forge a small colony on Madagascar, but it soon failed. French efforts to settle the island were likewise unsuccessful. Notorious pirates from various countries also began using Madagascar as an Indian Ocean base of operations. Generally, Europeans found the island people not particularly welcoming—and the coastal waters treacherous.

Although France did not establish itself on Madagascar, in 1669 French settlers occupied Réunion, a small island several hundred miles to the east. France claimed not only Réunion but Madagascar as key pieces of its island holdings, though other countries disputed French authority over Madagascar. England, for example, recognized Madagascar as an independent domain around 1800. Nevertheless, the French in time gained an actual foothold on Madagascar. In the early 1800s they built a factory and engaged island workers. Within a few years, they had established a small industrial city.

England meanwhile forged a bond with King Radama I, the island's most powerful leader of the early nineteenth century. Radama allowed the English to set up mission posts and schools. Unhappily for the British, Radama's successor was Queen Ranavalona I, who despised the English and favored the French.

In the mid 1880s, as the European powers began "carving up" Africa, France made Madagascar one of its "protectorates." A few years later, England formally gave up its claims of control. Madagascar became a French colony in 1895. Joseph Simon Gallieni was appointed governor-general, and French became the colony's official language.

The missionaries on Madagascar, as across Africa, established western-style schooling. Beginning in 1820 missionaries began opening schools for Malagasy children and printing the New Testament in the Malagasy language. Mission work was blocked for three decades during the reign of Queen Ranavalona, who feared that education and Christian gatherings diminished her control. Missionaries were expelled, Christianity was banned, and all but a select few of the inhabitants were forbidden to learn to read or write. Mission work resumed after her death in 1861.

Three Girls, Rhodesia, c. 1896 *Rhodesia was known for its elaborate textiles. Elderly men, who no longer had the strength to hunt, monopolized the weaving of raffia palm cloth. Textile production was important to native chiefs for trade. Also, cloth provided one of the more durable and valuable possessions. In particular, bride wealth—which in other parts of Africa might be paid in gold or cattle—was commonly paid in cloth.*

3

LIFE IN COLONIAL SOUTHEAST AFRICA

Whenjournalist O.W. Barrett visited Mozambique around 1910, he found "four or five good ports and as many bad ones; five towns and a small but up-to-date capital city; and a generous number of military posts and out-posts, a few of which are in the real raw interior." He described vast expanses of fertile land "fairly aching to show the farmer what big crops may be grown."

The country was nearly perfect, as he saw it, with no deserts, "mountainous wastes," or "impenetrable jungles" to hinder settlement. Just as important was the unresisting nature of the people. Barrett estimated there were "only one or two tribes that object seriously to paying taxes to the government, now that they realize that the tax collector is a vital organ of the white tribe, which objects to any one tribe extermi-nating another in the good old way."

As Barrett pointed out, the European colonists' perspective of Southeast Africa was that here was a land of beauty and promise just waiting for Europeans to come and tame. But it was a land with hardships and challenges as well. Simply traveling in many parts of the region posed difficulties. "The traveler in Madagascar," wrote American scientist Charles F. Swingle in 1929, "needs not only to protect his head from the blistering heat of the sun and his eyes from its blinding rays, but if he enters the brush he must take care that his legs are well fortified against the vicious thorns."

Once they got to where they were going, European visitors learned to expect much less than the conveniences to which they were accustomed at home. "Rumors of good accommodations in Tuléar," Swingle quipped, "had led us to look forward to a few days' rest before forging ahead into the desert, but the Grand Hotel proved to be grand only in name; its two rooms were already occupied!"

One of Swingle's modes of travel was the much-less-than-comfortable *filanzana*. "It consists of a chair swung on two 10-foot poles, and is carried on the shoulders of four stalwart natives. These alternate every five minutes with four others, so that a filanzana crew consists of eight men. Thus we had 16 porters whose sole duty it was to carry my companion and me."

Interestingly, Swingle reported that the lot of the filanzana bearer—who was paid 12 cents daily—was not considered a lowly one at all. "[A]s he trots along his laughing and chattering never cease. To his mind it is an honor to be one of the filanzana crew, and his contempt for the lowly baggage carrier is very amusing."

Western visitors were startled at the living conditions in some areas, which straddled the very line between life and death. Wrote Swingle in southern Madagascar: "We hoped to replenish our water supply at one of several villages which lay in our path, but in each of these tiny communities, boasting not more than a dozen or so grass huts, we found the natives had barely enough water for their own needs. In fact, so precarious was their situation that women of the village were often seen collecting the early morning dew from the bushes on which it gathered during the night. This they did by beating the branches with heavy paddles, making sure that every bit of water fell into their thick clay jugs."

The water the scientists did manage to find on their expedition was bad, he added. "Not a drop was really drinkable, and we were glad to use our daily malaria preventive (quinine) to remove its foul taste from our mouths." At the same time, it was a place of incredible natural beauty and intrigue. "[T]his traveler's hell is surely a botanist's paradise," Swingle reasoned. "So abundant were the plants in this region that in most places it was impossible to penetrate the dense thickets, and we could move only along cut paths."

A Handful of Conquerors Infiltrate a Continent

The Europeans who colonized Africa were not merely a small minority of the continent's population; they were ridiculously outnumbered. American W. Robert Moore, reporting from Rhodesia in 1944—the late colonial era—observed, "Over the broad Rhodesian spaces white people are scattered so thinly as to make our emptiest State, Nevada, look filled by comparison. There are only about 89,000 Europeans in Southern Rhodesia, and 15,000 in the big Northern colony. There are about 26 black natives to every white person. It is still a young pioneer land."

Throughout the colonial era, blacks in Mozambique and Rhodesia always outnumbered whites by at least 20 to 1. Yet the whites controlled. In Southern Rhodesia during the 1960s, for example, whites owned almost half the land even though they represented less than 5 percent of the population. And generally the whites lived in high style compared with the blacks. Melville Chater, chronicling a journey through Rhodesia in 1935, wrote,

> To reach a Rhodesian settler's farmstead, you might possibly drive twenty wooded miles off the turnpike, and, if it is after nightfall, hear some stray lion gulping gutturally in the distance. Yet, once arrived, you find yourself in a true home that the man and his wife have made together. He and his native boys have built the house, planning it around a big central room with a wide hearth. She has made it bright with gay curtains, with the rugs brought from overseas, with the homeland's flowers.

Native Man, Rhodesia, c. 1896 *The textile trade of Rhodesia was controlled by local chiefs who supplied protection to the caravanners. Raffia palm cloth had a velvetlike pile, and it was produced in a rich range of natural colors.*

And the smart furniture? Well, Rhodesia has its teak, and it is astonishing what carpentry native "boys" can achieve with the assistance of designs cut from household magazines, and the vicarious elbow grease of your constant presence.

Across the broad acres the reaped corn stands in regimental stacks. There's a farm store where the settler sells to his native "boys." For amusements, there are horseback riding, hunting, and fishing, books from public libraries, and maybe a radio set.

As for educating the regional settlers' children, a minimum of ten pupils calls for the establishment of a governmental school. Failing that number, in sparsely peopled sections, there will be an "aided farm school," with a Government grant for each child.

Yet, the European settlers were widespread and isolated, and they knew it. The roads were not the best, and dangerous wildlife often added to the hazards of travel, as Chater described:

Fortunately, our native chauffeur knew the roads, for at times we traversed fifty miles of wild woodland that offered no more guiding features than a dry streambed or some cement causeway, built at low level to allow seasonal torrents to sweep across instead of under it. Brilliantly plumaged birds flashed past, groups of rock-perched baboons discussed family affairs. Issuance into the open, with a mission church ahead, was an experience, while the passage of some other car was a downright sensation. . . .

Along the road we had noted the gnawed remains of a buck, and knew it portended that lions were about. Being without so much as a popgun, it was with eerie feelings that, some miles farther on, we descried a lion *couchant* on a mound by the roadside. The road was uncomfortably narrow, the lion was uncomfortably large. We stopped at a respectful distance, behind a screen of brush, and waited for his majesty to move on. But move he would not.

The impasse ended happily for all when one of the motorists came up with the notion (and the nerve) of sneaking upwind of the lion and leaving a meal of smelly ham sandwiches. Chater concluded, "Ten minutes later, the recumbent monarch lifted his head, showed interest, appeared to sniff the air; then he stalked down from the mound and disappeared, leaving our way free."

The Portuguese in Mozambique maintained control in important trading areas by making minor government officials of village chiefs. The Africans played key roles in daily administration (law enforcement, local court systems, labor management), but operated beneath a Portuguese official.

A tiny fraction of the Mozambique people mastered the Portuguese language and adopted Portuguese customs. Called *assimilados*, they came to be almost equal to Portuguese nationals in class and privileges.

Big Game, Big Games

R.C.F. Maugham was British consul to Portuguese East Africa at the beginning of the twentieth century. One of the pleasant fascinations he observed in his journeys was the way Africans entertained themselves. He wrote,

> "Dancing and singing are the principal forms of native
> amusement, and are indulged in all over the country
> about the time of full moon. The music of the drums is
> the most general form of accompaniment, and many of
> the people become astonishingly expert in beating them.
> The num-ber of drums used at one time is as a rule three,
> and this number is never allowed to exceed five or six,
> although
> on one occasion, when I was in Maravi's main town, close
> to Mozambique, I witnessed a dance in which over 2,000
> persons took part, to music furnished by over thirty
> drums . . . "

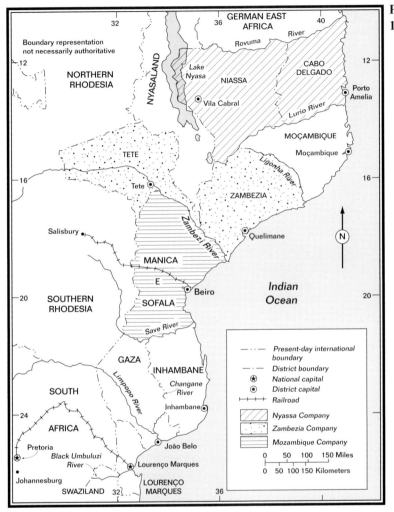

Portuguese Mozambique, 1907

O.W. Barrett, a visitor to Mozambique in 1910, witnessed a *batuque* or ball, that attracted 3,000 people and lasted almost three days. "To describe the weird minor music of the marimbas, or huge xylophones, the blood-freezing death chants, the thrilling war songs, the 'expression' dances of both women and men, and the rites and divination ceremonies which the witch doctors were induced to show us would require much space," he wrote. Later, he saw an even bigger festival attended by people of several

African groups. An estimated 200 marimbas "kept up an incessant din for 36 hours. The 'tunes' varied with the tribes. The Portuguese national air was executed pretty well by several of the bands, who had picked it up from obscure sources." He continued,

> The warriors in the dance, who may number 300 or more, constantly drop in their tracks and pretend to be smitten with death. The witch doctor then passes around, sprinkling them with medicine, whereupon all gradually resume their places and the dance continues. This dance is said to be as old as the tribe, which is probably the oldest Kafir tribe in East Africa . . .
>
> The young girls' dance of the M'chopi tribe requires several years' practice before the difficult poses and contortions can be successfully performed.

At these widely attended gatherings, Barrett observed, "the tribes meet but do not mingle."

An even greater marvel for the Europeans was the big game they encountered. Wrote Barrett,

> On the Zambesi, at the head of Chinde, I counted eight hippos at one time around the boat. Since the natives are not supposed to have guns of any sort, and since few devastating tourists pass that way, these uncouth monsters may endure a few years longer. There are usually to be seen one or two pairs in the Inkomati River, some three hours from Lourenco Marques, the capital. Feet a foot across and a body as wide as a wagon—no wonder the poor native sits up nights beside his corn-field when he hears the ominous "woo-uff" of an old tramp bull in the neighborhood.

The dangers wild animals posed to the human population were not exaggerated. On the same trip, Barrett reported,

> Near Mopea, three days up the Zambesi, we passed through two small native kraals [villages] in which the lions had

eaten 18 people in three months previous. It is quite impossible to hunt these man-eaters on account of the tall, rank grass (four to six feet high), and, since they soon learn that two or three cuffs will make a big hole in the side of an ordinary hut, the poor native must roost high or die.

Even Major Kirby, the famous lion hunter, has not been able, he tells me, to average one lion per month during his stay in the Boror Company's estates, where over 100 people were devoured last year.

Barrett was impressed by the honesty and friendliness of the people of Mozambique. Not once during his ten weeks in the territory was anything stolen from his party, nor did the visitors ever feel it necessary to punish any of their bearers and guides. (White explorers in Africa were notorious for brutalizing their local helpers for even small or imagined misbehavior.) In fact, Barrett said, "the farther away from civilized centers we went, the more respectable became the native."

Exploring a Vast Island

Swingle was an American botanist who in the late 1920s, with a fellow scientist, embarked on a 1,300-mile "plant hunt" through southern Madagascar—an area "richly endowed yet grimly fortified by Nature." Because of its rugged remoteness, much of the Madagascar interior was unexplored by scientists at the time. In fact, getting across the country from Mahajanga, the port where they landed, was an adventure for Swingle and his companion. For three days they were cramped "aboard frail river craft, which meandered slowly up the brick-red waters of the Betsiboka to the nearest bus terminal. . . . Throughout this part of our trip the best we could do was to trust that our tiny, overloaded boats would not be wrecked on one of the numerous snags in the river, for the water all along was teeming with crocodiles, ranging from cunning little fellows a couple of feet long to monsters of 16 or 18 feet."

Woman, Rhodesia, c. 1896
*The photographer simply
titled this image "Portrait."*

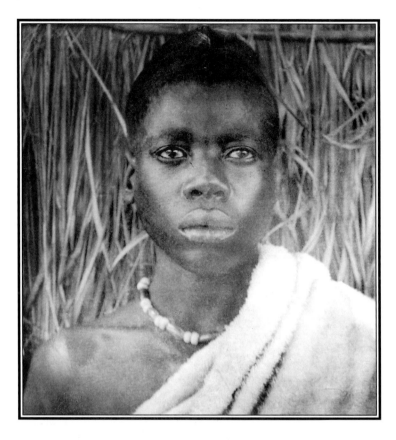

Then they boarded a bus, which "the natives looked upon . . . with a combination of wonder and fear. The driver had only to sound his horn to send frightened pedestrians scurrying in every direction. Once out of harm's way, they would swing around and join in a whole-hearted laugh."

Cattle were everywhere to be found—but they were not such a food staple as rice. Recorded Swingle,

Madagascar boasts that it has more cattle per capita than any other country in the world, and far more important to the native than a bank account, a bag of jewels, or a fine home is his herd of humpback zebus; for these bespeak his wealth and influence as nothing else could. He would much prefer to let his wife and children go hungry than to sell one of his precious herd. To kill a beef for food is unthinkable, and it is only at taxpaying time that he is forced to slaughter some of his animals and sell their hides to obtain cash.

Excitement regularly was in the air on market day. Swingle wrote,

The *zoma*, or market, at Tananarive [Antananarivo, the island's capital] is one of the most interesting sights in Madagascar. On market day, in from the country stream the natives, walking for miles, bringing their wares with them, balancing their loads upon their heads—baskets of eggs and rice, piles of bright-colored mats, live chickens and geese . . .

At the Tananarive market I was able to buy few of the articles which civilization had taught me to depend upon. However, I saw a myriad of things which bring joy and delight to the Malagash—piles of wearing apparel of a forgotten European style, strange and doubtful native medicines, baskets of locusts, empty bottles, and tin cans. . . . I made daily trips to the market to procure peanuts, bananas, pineapples, guavas, loquats, mangoes, oranges, and papayas with which to supplement our hotel diet.

I was told that the Malagash language has in it no word for time; a glimpse at the market tends to confirm this. Here the native, after spending a day or so walking to town, is content to sit waiting several days for a customer to buy the armful of wood or the chicken he has brought to market. Once in possession of the few cents his goods have sold for, he carefully selects a prize from the many lots of clothing or trinkets on display and happily wends his way homeward, feeling very grand in the derby hat, the overcoat, or other bit of finery he has purchased.

Like Africans in the remoter parts of the mainland during the colonial era, the Malagasy experienced little change from the lifestyles of their ancestors. In Antananarivo, the capital, simple brick homes covered the hillsides. One conspicuous structure in an otherwise inconspicuous city was the "Palace of the Queen." After the French occupation and the exile of the island's last queen, the royal palace in Antananarivo was made into a Malagasy museum.

"When one enters a one-room Malagash home, stooping low in order to get through the tiny doorway, he sees little in the way of furniture," wrote Swingle. "A large mat on the floor, a fireplace with no outlet for the smoke, a few baskets of rice, a large iron pot for cooking it, one or two earthen jugs or large calabashes [gourdlike utensils] for water, and the Malagash home is complete—or almost so. Of course, to be really fashionable, it must have a few good-luck charms and beautiful cast-off trinkets about. Nor must I fail to mention the sooty cobwebs which, hanging in festoons from the ceiling, give the place its air of permanence."

Swingle described his awe at seeing a cloud of locusts. "It was a real swarm indeed, blackening the sky, and it took several hours for this dark cloud to pass. I had been told that locusts were greatly esteemed by the natives for food, and a little bit later, at the big public market in Tananarive, I saw scores of bushels of these choice viands on sale."

A Short-Lived Fantasy

The last thing colonial officials wanted to see was unity among the African peoples. They encouraged and sometimes forced divisions within a colony. In Zambia, for example, the British identified more than seventy tribal groups. As mentioned earlier, the white administrators supported individual chiefs. In this way, they fostered the allegiance of local African leaders—and hence of the people.

Colonial administrations were devoted primarily to the interests of the ruling country's citizens who settled in Africa. They built railroads and developed road systems not so much for the Africans as for the colonists. They helped whites grow and sell cash crops but did little to encourage agriculture among the original inhabitants. It was true that they pressured the chiefs to end slavery and brutal customs, but they drew a clear line of distinction between the races in colonial society.

In general, Africans did not respond violently in the early years of white rule. Rather, they did their best to adjust. "Having resisted the colonial invaders in vain," wrote historian Basil Davidson, "Africans naturally looked for ways of getting a place inside the new systems, or even of turning these systems to African advantage." But the effort was bound to fail, for most Africans. "They were too poor or powerless to join the social groups, or the 'better-off classes'. . . . The new ways of working and earning kept them fixed in their poverty and ignorance; the gains of colonial rule passed them by. For them, the choice was a hard one: to give in, or to revolt."

Tension was always there, but many white colonists in Southeast Africa during the early 1900s believed their own prospects were bright. There were obstacles to overcome—notably, diseases that decimated both humans and cattle—and much work to be done before big profits could be realized. "But the steam plow has put in its appearance," O.W. Barrett wrote cheerily from Mozambique in 1910, "and as soon as permanent regulations for sale or rental of land are promulgated the country should be a happy harvesting ground for planters. With labor at $2 to $5 per month, good transportation, no more sickness than in any other country, perhaps, and good support from the government, colonists will come and then Mozambique will gloriously come into her own."

Such was the white planters' optimism. They certainly could count on cheap African labor, improved transportation, and support from the colonial governments—factors which were not so promising to native Africans. When the Southeast African colonies did "come into their own" in the mid-twentieth century, it was not in a way Barrett or other westerners would have imagined in 1910.

Killed hippos, Northeast Rhodesia

4

INDEPENDENCE

As far as most Europeans understood the situation in Africa, their colonial officers were doing a wonderful job, a thankless job, bringing "civilization" to a savage people. They could not imagine letting the Africans go unguided by western learning and innovation.

In his report from Mozambique, chronicler O.W. Barrett stated in 1910, "The colonization laws are pronounced excellent, even by English colonials. [Mozambique was a Portuguese colony at the time.] They are automatic—just to the government, to the colonist, and to the natives. And here I may say that it seems to be agreed by men who know that nowhere else in Africa is the native question so well managed as in Mozambique. But it is a very big and deep and difficult question."

Some of the other territories in Africa certainly had posed more problems for the European overlords than Mozambique by that point in the colonial era. It was naïve to think the "native question," as Barrett termed it, was under control, however. It may have been quiet for a time, but it was a warming wind that soon would swirl into a tempest.

It wasn't just the segregationist, supremacist attitude of the Europeans that stirred the Africans to action, or even the simple, maddening thought that an unwelcome foreign regime was claiming sovereignty over the land. In practical matters, the colonists were making a difficult life even more difficult for the original inhabitants. One example: The white Rhodesian administration forbade Africans from selling their cattle at market. The government claimed livestock raised outside white-controlled farms often was diseased. Blacks thus had only one way to earn money for their herds—sell them to white cattlemen at cut rates. The whites then could sell the same livestock at full price in the markets. Apparently, the government's logic was that by passing through white ownership, the potentially infected cattle miraculously were cleansed and thus fit for public sale. In reality, it was one more way in which the whites maintained a good living at the expense of blacks.

Not lost on Africans, meanwhile, was the obvious fact that most of the land on or near the rail lines belonged to European settlers. That made it easy for the Europeans to market what they grew. "In the early 1920's," noted historian Robin Hallett, "by far the greater part of the country's [Rhodesia's] exports was produced on the estates of European planters. . . . "

Black miners in Rhodesia fared no better than farmers. They had jobs, it was true. But the pay was low and workers' housing in the mining towns abysmal. Black miners in the copper belt during the 1930s were paid about one-twenty-fifth as much as Europeans. Many of the African workers were poorly fed. In return for the privilege of laboring long hours in these questionable circumstances, the native miners had to pay stiff taxes. Again, it was a situation in which the colonial regime found many ways to take advantage of Africans. Here, they obtained very cheap labor to extract the natural wealth of the land for white mining interests.

TROUBLE FOR THE PORTUGUESE

One of the factors that triggered early nationalistic movements across Africa was World War I (1914–1918). As a battleground, Africa was little more than a sideshow of the great conflict. The war impacted Africans dramatically, however, as the various European powers pressed colonial citizens into service. Thousands of African soldiers fought side by side with Europeans—free Europeans.

Why should they fight for the white man's strange causes? Most African soldiers never dared raise the question, but they couldn't fail to wonder. And at home, fledgling political activists were pressing the issue. Violent protests were staged in Mozambique in 1917.

Portuguese police—and secret police—controlled the coastal colony with a heavy hand. Repressed, and unable to earn a living under the colonial system, some half-million Africans had relocated to other colonies by the mid 1900s. The trend of leaving Mozambique, by either legal or illegal means, continued to the end of the century.

Because of secret police pressure inside the colony, political organizations working for an independent Mozambique organized outside the country. Emerging at the forefront was the Front for the Liberation of Mozambique, also called Frelimo, created by the merger of three factions in 1962 and led by Eduardo Mondlane. The independence movement in Mozambique turned bloody in 1964, with Frelimo forces battling Portuguese soldiers and police. Frelimo established control in northern Mozambique; the Portuguese government held firm in the south. Although the liberation movement attracted a broad base of popular support and funds from other countries, it was alarmingly factional.

Mozambique's civil war lasted into the 1970s. Many Frelimo leaders were killed, including Mondlane, who was assassinated with a letter bomb.

Portugal could ill afford to deal with rebellion in a distant colony. Indeed, the home country itself faced the threat of revolution—which actually came to pass in 1974. A military coup seized control in Lisbon, Portugal's capital. The new government moved quickly to give up control of its African colonies: Mozambique, Angola, and Guinea-Bissau. Independence day in Mozambique was June 25, 1975.

Independence placed power in the hands of the powerful Frelimo, which created a Marxist-style government radically different from that of the colony. Samora Machel, president of Frelimo, became Mozambique's first president.

THE DIVIDED COLONY

Both Northern and Southern Rhodesia prospered during the first half of the twentieth century, largely on the strength of mining operations. Copper exports from Northern Rhodesia, for example, were setting world records by the 1950s. The primary beneficiaries were not the black Africans who lived and worked there, but the white settlers.

In the south, the native Shona people were industrious farmers, while the Ndebele were remarkable cattlemen. It was the Europeans, though, who benefited most from millions of acres of prime Rhodesian farmland. More than 100,000 whites had been drawn to Southern Rhodesia by the mid 1950s. Using cheap black labor, Europeans became wealthy by producing such crops as tobacco and tea for world markets. In the meantime, tens of thousands of blacks were relegated to reserves to eke out a living. Those who worked on the white-run farms had no property rights.

The British in Rhodesia officially allowed natives to vote, but they set such high educational and economic requirements that few blacks could qualify. Racial segregation was marked, and virtually all the power was in the hands of whites. Resistance was inevitable.

In 1934 educated natives in Southern Rhodesia formed a fledgling division of the African National Congress (ANC), a growing nationalist movement on the continent. After struggling for popular support for two decades, the faction gained prominence in Southern Rhodesia—and was banned by the colonial government. In the early 1960s one of its leaders, Joshua Nkomo, helped form the Zimbabwe African People's Union (ZAPU), which likewise was outlawed. White settlers, meantime, were represented by the Rhodesian Front, a political movement devoted to preserving European power in the colony.

Rev. Ndabaningi Sithole in 1963 led the organization of a new native political force, the Zimbabwe African National Union (ZANU). It was a militant offshoot of the underground ZAPU. The colonial government, alarmed, arrested nationalist leaders.

In copper-rich Northern Rhodesia, black miners after World War II boldly opposed the colonial system of racial discrimination that doomed them to the lowest-paying jobs and no real voice in national affairs. They formed a union. Meanwhile, the ANC pressed for an end to white control, and a more powerful group, the United National Independence Party (UNIP), was organized in 1958.

Great Britain in 1953 created the Central African Federation, joining the administrations of Northern and Southern Rhodesia and Nyasaland. To black citizens, this seemed to be a diplomatic strategy for white-controlled Southern Rhodesia to expand control. Powerful whites in Southern Rhodesia, on the other hand, sensed the coming of majority rule for the whole area. Neither race trusted the other. Tension mounted, resulting in riots in 1959 in Nyasaland and Northern Rhodesia. The federation was dissolved in 1963.

The next year, Northern Rhodesia gained independence as the Republic of Zambia. Kenneth David Kaunda, a UNIP leader, became its first president. Although many whites moved away after independence, a few remained. Whites continue to work in Zambia today, most notably in farming operations. Zambia also has a minority of citizens of Asian descent.

Unlike other European holdings in colonial Africa, Southern Rhodesia (like South Africa) had come to be governed not so much by the home country as by the increasingly powerful white settler class. The whites in Southern Rhodesia put much of their own wealth back into the local economy. They literally had a "vested interest" in the affairs of their adopted homeland. Thus, long after the zest for colonial dominion had faltered in England, the white settlers of Southern Rhodesia stubbornly clung to control. Entering the decade of the 1960s, they came under growing criticism not only from the black majority where they were, but from outside nations, including England, which by that time generally favored majority government in Africa.

LATTER-DAY RHODESIA: BASTION OF WHITE RULE

In 1965 the white Rhodesian Front in Southern Rhodesia announced an independent nation, the Republic of Rhodesia. Its leader, Prime Minister Ian Smith, contended that the British government in London had abandoned the interests of its own citizens in the colony. If the white settlers were to survive, he argued, they must take matters into their own hands.

In terms of self-government, this observation was correct. British leaders long before had realized Africa could not be held by foreign governments. Reluctantly but necessarily, they were turning their other colonies back over to the original inhabitants of the continent. The same must be done sooner or later in Rhodesia, statesmen in London well knew. However, white Rhodesians stubbornly disagreed. Although only a tiny minority of the population, they believed their country's thriving economy was strong enough to support them, free of British influence. They genuinely felt Rhodesia was "their" country. (The fact that they were living on land their grandparents had wrested from the Africans seemed to be of little consideration.)

The declaration of white independence not only incensed the country's African majority; it brought international opposition. Universally, the world community refused to recognize the new republic, and the United Nations imposed a boycott of the country's exports. By the end of 1975 black militant groups were waging guerrilla warfare in the north, and Rhodesia's neighbors were actively supporting internal opposition to the government. Rebels were operating out of Zambia and Mozambique, just across the border. Rhodesia literally was being battered from almost every side, militarily and economically. Within three years, ZAPU and ZANU forces occupied most of Rhodesia.

More than a decade of negotiations failed to defuse the Rhodesian crisis. Finally, British Prime Minister Margaret Thatcher set up renewed talks in 1979. The result was the end of the white regime. British-supervised elections in 1980 made ZANU leader Robert Mugabe prime minister of the independent nation of Zimbabwe. Some 27,000 people had died during the years of civil strife.

ZAMBIA WAVERS

Zambia, to the north, had begun its era of independence with prosperity and promise. It was earning money from its copper mines and farms, building new schools and improving health care. The state of the nation soon began to deteriorate, however, as Zambia felt the effects of warfare in neighboring countries, particularly Rhodesia.

At the same time, Zambian President Kaunda became dictatorial. His administration imposed a one-party, socialist political system. Secret police arrested Kaunda's political opponents and the government became corrupt. Pressured to return to democracy, Kaunda allowed national elections in 1991. The UNIP party was defeated soundly, and labor leader Frederick Chiluba became president.

FREEDOM AND UPHEAVAL FOR NYASALAND

Dissension in Nyasaland (now Malawi) was evident as early as World War I. During that conflict in 1915, an African preacher named John Chilembwe led an uprising in Blantyre, protesting the involvement of black Africans in the Europeans' war.

Educated in America, Chilembwe had returned to his homeland at the beginning of the twentieth century to teach African workers and try to improve their situation under colonial rule. He became increasingly resentful toward the white regime during the early 1900s. When Britain drafted blacks and forced them to fight and die during the world war, Chilembwe protested, first verbally, then by leading an armed rebellion.

Chilembwe's revolt was small-scale and short-lived, ending in his death at the hands of Nyasaland police. But the seeds of nationalism had been sewn in Nyasaland and elsewhere in the region. Several independence movements and labor unions were afoot by the late 1940s. During the 1950s Nyasaland was the scene of a growing number of protests and riots; they became so alarming that the government administration declared a state of emergency in 1959.

By that time, the clear realization among colonial officials in Nyasaland, as in other colonies, was that Africa must be returned to the Africans—and soon. They agreed to hold legislative elections. The leading nationalistic party, the Nyasaland African Congress, won the majority of seats.

In 1964, the year after the Central African Federation (Northern and Southern Rhodesia and Nyasaland) was disbanded, Nyasaland gained its independence. It became the Republic of Malawi in 1966. Hastings Kamuzu Banda, a leader of the nationalist movement in the country during the 1950s and early 1960s, became the first prime minister and in 1971 was made "president for life." Banda's quarter-century of leadership was notable for political restrictions. In 1994 the country insisted on a free presidential election involving opposition parties. Bakili Muluzi defeated Banda and remained in office as of late 2001.

MADAGASCAR OUSTS THE FRENCH

On the island of Madagascar, political resistance to the French colonial administration was organized as early as 1913. A secret society called the Vy Vato Sakelika, consisting of educated Malagasy, made the French regime so uncomfortable that hundreds of its members were thrown in jail. Fuel was added to the nationalistic fire on Madagascar, as it was in other African colonies, when native citizens were urged to serve for France in World Wars I and II.

After the Second World War, France began a shift in policy that permitted the people of Madagascar to assume a degree of self-control. For one thing, France's "colony" was made a foreign "territory" with its own native representatives in Paris. Eager for independence, Malagasy leaders formed political parties. There was no immediate unification, however, and in 1947 mounting political tensions boiled into active unrest and violence. Thousands of people were killed, many others jailed.

Soon after Charles de Gaulle was elected president of France in 1958, his government began granting independence to overseas French colonies. Madagascar's independence came in June 1960. Philibert Tsiranana, a politician who kept close ties with France, was the first president. But over the next twelve years, the island gradually distanced itself from its French colonial heritage.

Nahue village

5

SOUTHEAST AFRICA AFTER INDEPENDENCE

The great tragedy of modern Africa is that almost invariably, its nations at their time of independence were not prepared to solve the plethora of problems they faced. Three generations of colonialism had left them weak and, in many situations, dangerously divided. In the main, they were poorly developed nations thrust into a world of highly developed ones.

For most of their new leaders, the first order of business was not to solve problems but simply to secure power. This they accomplished, all too frequently, with force and the repression of political opponents. Dictators rose—and often fell— in military coups that sometimes were peaceful but more often were bloody and traumatic.

How have the southeastern nations fared since independence? As a region, they have experienced far less explosive change than elsewhere on the continent. But that's not to suggest each country does not confront its unique set of monstrous problems.

Let's look at their recent histories, one by one. In doing so, we'll learn something of the life of the people in these nations as they enter the twenty-first century.

MADAGASCAR

Madagascar is the fourth largest island on earth (not counting the Australian continent), after Greenland, New Guinea, and Borneo. More than 350 miles wide and almost 1,000 miles long, it is believed to have broken away from the African continent in one of the planet's geologic upheavals millions of years ago. It's situated in the Indian Ocean some 250 miles off the coast of Mozambique.

Most of the Malagasy—the people of Madagascar—are small-scale farmers, and rice is their principal crop. They also grow and export coffee, sugar, pepper, cloves, vanilla, *sisal*, and other goods. Madagascar and nearby islands supply much of the world's vanilla, although production declined radically during the 1990s. It also is a leading supplier of farm-raised shrimp.

Yet, here, as throughout Africa, *subsistence farming*, in which farmers grow only what they need to live, is the norm. About five percent of the land is planted in crops; much more is used for grazing cattle. Commonly seen around the island are a species of humpbacked cows called zebu.

In the first decade of its independence, Madagascar was hit hard economically by a devastating cattle disease. The country also endured tensions between many of its coastal and interior dwellers. President Philibert Tsiranana in 1972 relinquished power to the military and three years later an army officer named Didier Ratsiraka became head of state. In 1975 Ratsiraka formally was elected president.

Ratsiraka made Madagascar practically a closed country, patterning his government after the communistic regime of North Korea. The government took control of most manufacturing, transportation, banking, and other businesses. The island's economy faltered. After two decades of Ratsiraka rule, the people elected a new leader, Albert Zafy, in 1992. Zafy was unable to assume full control, however. He was impeached in 1996, and Ratsiraka—apparently with a more open-minded strategy of government after his temporary banishment—was restored to the presidency.

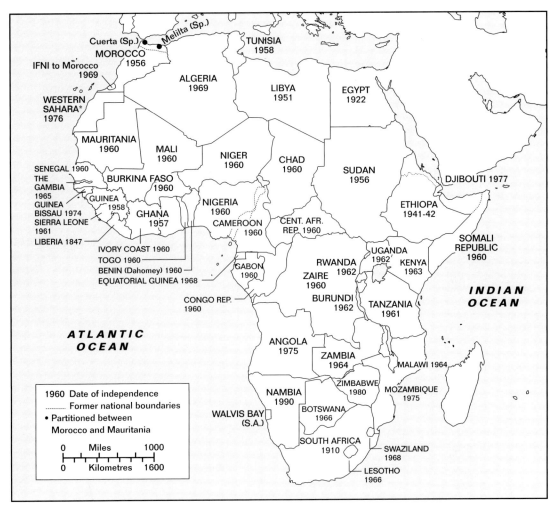

Africa after Independence, 1991

Malagasy children are required to attend school for five years. Sadly, only a small percentage go on to higher education. More than half the citizens of Madagascar are younger than seventeen; only about 3 percent are older than sixty-five; the average life expectancy is early fifties. Unsanitary conditions in some parts of Madagascar pose public health problems. Bad drinking water in recent years has contributed to the spread of cholera, a disease that can be fatal.

Slightly more than half the Malagasy continue their traditional religious beliefs, which hold that dead ancestors impact the living. Ornately carved and painted tombs among upper-class families are signs of their reverence for dead forebears. About 40 percent are Christians, following the faith brought by Catholic and Protestant missionaries beginning in the 1600s. Most of the remainder are Muslims.

In recent years Madagascar has drawn the concern of environmentalists. They fear its farmers and timber cutters have cleared forests and open areas for planting too rapidly to let the land adapt. One marked result has been erosion, which has washed vast quantities of the island's mineral-rich soil into the sea.

Antananarivo, a city near the heart of the island with more than a million inhabitants, is the capital. Both French and Malagasy are considered official languages.

MALAWI

The Banda government of Malawi during the 1960s and 1970s was extremely cautious and restrictive. For example, it enacted laws governing the length of men's hair and the style and cut of women's clothing. Even visitors to the country were required to follow the national dress code.

Since independence, Malawi has been a nation of relative peace, although it has been caught up in the conflicts and issues of its neighbors. A longstanding dispute with Tanzania involved shoreline claims along northern Lake Malawi. Malawi was one of the rare nations to maintain ties with South Africa during the latter years of apartheid—a stand that caused serious dissention among Malawi's African citizens. Watchdog organizations have criticized Malawi for human rights abuses entering the twenty-first century.

A relatively small nation of some 12 million people, the Republic of Malawi lies along the west bank of Lake Nyasa. Almost 90 percent of the country's people are small-scale farmers living in remote hut villages. Corn is their main food. The lake, naturally, is the source of an important fishing industry.

Lion shot on Urama Plain

Although Lake Malawi is a good provider for the country that shares its name, the remote location has hampered Malawi's progress among the world of nations. Transportation and commerce to and from many parts of the country are not easily managed. Most of Malawi's roads are dirt; some are impassable in muddy conditions.

At independence, masses of workers from Malawi were living in South Africa and other mining regions to the south, where they found employment their own nation could not offer. Within fifteen years, however, most of them were able to return home and find jobs.

Some two-thirds of the country's people follow the Christian faith. Ancestral religions and Islam are the leading minorities. David Livingstone and the missionaries who followed him established Christianity in the area during the late 1800s, but during the colonial era a strong independent Christian movement spread among their converts. Islam was introduced to the Lake Malawi locale by an Arab slave trader during the 1860s.

The traditional African religion is *animist* in nature, holding that spirits live in certain rocks, trees, and other objects.

Health care and education in Malawi were serious problems as the new republic made its way through the first half century of independence. With only a handful of doctors to serve them, people often died of illnesses that easily were curable in western countries—measles, stomach disorders, malnourishment, for example. The infant mortality rate was 17 percent, and the average life expectancy for Malawians was only in the mid forties. Current health threats include AIDS, which threatens all classes of people.

Schools and teachers were woefully insufficient to serve the population during the first decades of independence. The literacy rate was a doleful 25 percent.

Malawi has both a "national language," Chichewa (a Bantu tongue), and an "official language," English. Lilongwe, lying in the western plateau region, is Malawi's capital. Blantyre, situated in the far south near the Mozambique border, is the largest city, with a population of about a half million.

MOZAMBIQUE

As we saw in the previous chapter, guerrilla forces battled the Portuguese administration for more than ten years leading up to Mozambique's independence in 1975. More than 90 percent of the white residents left—a departure of some 150,000 people. Mozambique became a socialist nation based on the systems of communist Russia and China. Hundreds of communes were created, and large farming operations, businesses, and industries were nationalized.

Ironically, the Frelimo organization, which had won a great victory over oppression in its civil war against the Portuguese secret police and military, itself became a political party of oppression. Thousands of people were jailed for unproved crimes. Religious activities were opposed.

A weak nation from the outset, Mozambique had to recover not only from guerrilla warfare but from fighting on its western border with Rhodesia (soon to become Zimbabwe). As whites were ousted from large plantations, farm production plummeted. For several years during the late 1970s Mozambique closed its western border with Rhodesia, interrupting commercial and transportation revenues.

President Samora Machel's Frelimo government, meanwhile, was opposed strongly by a group called the Renamo. Renamo rebels destroyed buildings and terrorized citizens who supported the government. Fighting between the two political forces devastated the new nation's economy. More than a million people fled to neighboring Malawi, South Africa, and other countries. Another million died in the violence or starved to death.

When Machel died in a 1986 plane crash, Foreign Minister Joaquim Alberto Chissano became president. Chissano and the Renamo leader, Afonso Dhlakama, began to make overtures for peace. After more than a decade of destruction and killing, the sides agreed to a cease-fire in 1990 and signed a formal peace accord two years later. Meanwhile, Mozambique in 1990 abandoned communism and established a free economic and government system.

Recovery from its civil war took years. An immediate problem was the existence of an estimated 2 million live land mines that had been planted by the opposing armies. The location of some of the minefields had been forgotten. They had to be found and removed before Mozambique's throngs of refugees safely could return to their home country.

The war also left a large homeless population, including hundreds of thousands of orphaned children. Fighting and burning ruined the country's health care system, which already was struggling. The socialist Machel government had made it illegal for doctors to have private patients; most doctors therefore had left the country. Added to this dilemma was the destruction of health clinics during the conflict. The government in the 1990s changed the old law to allow doctors to establish private practices, and it began rebuilding clinics.

Mozambique also is trying to improve its educational system. Only about 10 percent of the citizens were literate when the country became independent in 1975. Schools were built and adult literacy courses developed. But, like the health clinics and other facilities, many schools were destroyed or damaged during the civil war.

Most Mozambique citizens farm, growing sisal, tea, grains, and other crops. In the early 1970s Mozambique produced more cashew nuts than any other country; production plummeted after independence because of the Machel regime's socialistic policies, but it recently has been on the increase.

Drought is not uncommon, threatening massive crop loss and famine. Completion in 1974 of a hydroelectric facility on the River Zambezi provided an enormous output of electrical power, but much of it went to industrial regions in the Transvaal section of South Africa.

Commercial and independent fishing along the coast and in the rivers is important to Mozambique's economy. Fish and shrimp are produced for both export and local consumption.

Approximately half of Mozambique's people hold traditional African religious beliefs. Most of the remainder are Christians and Muslims. The country's sixty-plus ethnic groups speak a number of indigenous languages as well as Portuguese, the official language.

Maputo (formerly called Lourenço Marques), a city of more than 2 million people, is Mozambique's capital and major port. Chissano continued to hold the presidency, now an elected position, as of late 2001.

ZAMBIA

Since restoring a democratic form of government in 1991, Zambians have enjoyed free political expression. But while the country's current constitution guarantees human rights, the state still exercises significant control. Its national broadcasting company and key newspapers are state organs, for example. President Frederick Chiluba's Movement for Multi-Party Democracy dominates the country's parliament.

Although the Chiluba government brought a welcome change from the Kaunda dictatorship, it, too, has come under criticism.

Observers have accused Chiluba's party of political oppression. A coup attempt failed in October 1997.

Zambia is one of the world's poorest countries, beleaguered by foreign debt and a growing population—approximately half its people range in age from infants to teens. Athough it is a fertile land, Zambia periodically endures droughts. These weather calamities hamper the country's agricultural potential, which is sorely underdeveloped. Most of the farming is done by poor villagers on small farms. These rural families strive to produce what they need to live on and hopefully generate a small amount of cash. The few large, modern farming operations situated along the rail lines cannot supply the rest of the country's demands. As a result, Zambia has to import much of its food.

Government mismanagement, in the long run, has hurt Zambian farmers worse than droughts. For example, Kaunda's administration required farmers to sell corn to the government at low prices so the government, in turn, could make the corn available cheaply to the masses in Zambia's cities and towns. Farmers discovered they could buy corn at lower prices in urban centers than it was costing them to produce it! Predictably, they began moving to town themselves. The result: agricultural output dropped.

Nine-tenths of Zambia's exports are mining products, most notably copper and cobalt. Otherwise, manufacturing has not prospered in Zambia. Small industries, however, export a variety of goods, from jewelry to cement, copper wire to bottled beer.

Like other African nations, Zambia faces the problems of growing human encroachment into the wild. *Poachers* who deal in ivory threaten the country's elephant population and almost have eliminated the rhinoceros. Some of the cities are overpopulated and marred by pollution; factory waste contaminates rivers; pesticides used by farmers have killed certain wildlife.

Educational facilities in Zambia are inadequate. Only a fraction of the country's young people proceed beyond primary instruction, and adult illiteracy is high. During the years immediately following independence, the government built new schools, technical colleges, and professional training facilities. Within a generation, though, the educational system had fallen into neglect.

The greatest health crisis of the late twentieth century in Zambia, as in many other African countries, was AIDS. In the late 1990s it was estimated that as many as a third of Zambia's teens and adults were HIV-positive (they carried the virus that causes AIDS), and half a million children had been orphaned by the plague.

Zambia's population is almost evenly divided between urban and rural dwellers. A number of groups still follow the leadership of chiefs, much like their ancestors did, although modern chiefs must be approved by the government.

The country's constitution proclaims it to be a Christian republic but guarantees the right to practice other faiths. Roman Catholicism is the dominant religion, despite the fact that the first missionaries in the region were Protestants. Certain "Africanist" churches combine Christianity with ancient native beliefs. Minority religions include Islam and Hindu, which gradually were introduced to the interior by Arab and Indian traders of old.

English is the official language. Zambians also speak a variety of traditional Bantu tongues, and individuals commonly speak several languages. Lusaka, located near the middle of the country, is Zambia's capital and a major air/rail/road hub of south-central Africa.

ZIMBABWE

Well into the 1970s—a decade after most other former African colonies had become independent nations—Europeans still were emigrating to Rhodesia. Farming and manufacturing thrived. Whites, the small minority of Rhodesians, were enjoying most of the prosperity.

Dismal living conditions among native blacks brought disfavor from foreign observers, however. Whites' insistence on keeping control at the expense of poorly paid African laborers eventually resulted in international trade sanctions. Rhodesia, like South Africa, became an isolated country, held in scorn by

Nahue village

much of the rest of the world. We saw in the last chapter how Zimbabwe—colonial Southern Rhodesia—became independent from minority white authority in 1980 after fifteen years of guerrilla warfare.

Rich in such minerals as chromium and asbestos, Zimbabwe began its independence as a relatively well-developed manufacturing nation; it still is one of Africa's most important mining countries, is a major coal producer, and operates a variety of industries. The British administration left it with good transportation and communication systems in place and a skilled labor force. But the new nation faced underlying problems of a spiraling population and high unemployment among native blacks. United Nations boycotts had damaged the economy under the old government, with lasting results. And like Mozambique, Zimbabwe's society had been disrupted dramatically by guerrilla warfare. The new regime of Robert Mugabe, a Marxist, divided much of the formerly white-owned property.

Cutting up buffalo, Mozambique, 1906

The new government promoted communal living. Mugabe remains president today.

Unity among Zimbabweans has been a challenge since independence. With the departure of the white minority government, power went to the Shona, by far the country's largest ethnic group. Minorities include the native Ndebele and the whites who remained after independence. English is Zimbabwe's official language. The most common native language group is Shona.

The government requires schooling for children under age fifteen. Higher learning centers provide vocational and college educations.

Like so much of Africa, Zimbabwe is the home of rich and varied wildlife. More than half the country is covered by forests. During the early colonial era, white hunters arrived, eagerly seeking rhinos, elephants, lions, and other major game. Today, Zimbabwe maintains a number of preserves—the result of a conservation movement begun before independence—to protect its animals. The largest, located near Victoria Falls, is Hwange National Park.

While it's one of Africa's strongest manufacturing areas, modern Zimbabwe, like its neighbors, is primarily an agricultural nation. Seventy percent of Zimbabwe's workers are employed in agriculture. Corn is the main crop; tobacco, cotton, grain, tea, and coffee also are important, and beef is a key export. An advantage Zimbabwe has enjoyed over other African countries has been its ability to produce ample food for its people and to export some of its produce, as well. Freshwater fisheries are a vital part of the country's food production.

City dwellers in Zimbabwe dress and work much like westerners. Harare, the capital, is one of Africa's most modern cities, with a skyline of tall buildings. Life for remote rural dwellers, by contrast, is much the same as it was for their forebears. They typically live in quaint huts and wear coarse cotton clothing.

For many centuries, Zimbabweans have held sacred the Matopos Hills, an area of boulder-topped highlands where ancient chiefs were buried.

Tradition Survives Tribulation

Noted African educator and commentator Ali A. Mazrui published a book in 1986 in which he voiced the frustrated conclusion of most observers regarding independent Africa: "Things are not working in Africa. From Dakar to Dar es Salaam, from Marrakesh to Maputo, institutions are decaying, structures are rusting away." The new Africa, Mazrui warned, had forgotten its own precolonial past and was struggling to modernize "without consulting cultural continuities." He pointed out that "what we regard as Africa today is primarily what Europeans decided was Africa."

Optimists take heart in the fact that despite the struggles to end colonialism and the sometimes catastrophic challenges of independence, Southeast Africa has emerged with many of its timeless traditions still in place. Its picture is not one of just hardships but also of joy and valuable contributions to humankind.

The meat rack, Zambia

The culture of Southeast Africa is vibrant. Much of it is based on age-old ballads, dance, storytelling, and art forms. Soccer and boxing are popular sports. Movies, television, and radio provide entertainment in urban centers. Rural dwellers enjoy sharing stories under a shade tree in the heat of the day or around the village fire in the evening. The oral tradition is especially active and important in Zimbabwe, where storytelling is a carefully memorized and practiced art form. Throughout the region, festivals and colorful parades are held on special days and draw large crowds.

Zimbabwe's fascinating pottery and other crafts come from a tradition dating to its ancient kingdom. Soapstone carvings are among the impressive relics of Great Zimbabwe. The country's people in recent times have come to appreciate western influences, as well. Here and in many other African countries, including Zambia and Malawi, pottery, leather and metal works, and other crafts and arts comprise a significant part of the livelihoods of many rural dwellers.

In Mozambique, basketry, wood carving and other crafts are as common today as they were in ages past. Among the most

Fontesvilla railway station, Mozambique

intriguing items are tall "family trees," ebony works that provide a type of visual storytelling. Painters, meanwhile, enjoy producing modern art works, which have become very popular in that country.

The island of Madagascar has a cultural heritage all its own. The Malagasy employ unique stringed and wind instruments in playing complicated folk music unfamiliar yet fascinating to western ears. Music is used to accompany a broad variety of dance forms.

Zimbabwe in the twentieth century produced important writers in the black nationalist movement. They included Wilson Katiyo, who was sent into exile during the turbulent white administration of Ian Smith in the 1970s, and Nobel Peace Prize winner Albert Luthuli.

Although new industries and methods are used in the twenty-first century, in Southeast Africa, people largely are following in the footsteps of the ancients. They farm, fish, and mine copper and other minerals that were mined by their ancestors hundreds of years ago. Universally—in any country's history—there is security in that kind of continuity.

WORLD WITHOUT END

DEIRDRE SHIELDS

ONE SUMMER'S DAY in 1830, a group of Englishmen met in London and decided to start a learned society to promote "that most important and entertaining branch of knowledge—Geography," and the Royal Geographical Society (RGS) was born.

The society was formed by the Raleigh Travellers' Club, an exclusive dining club, whose members met over exotic meals to swap tales of their travels. Members included Lord Broughton, who had travelled with the poet Byron, and John Barrow, who had worked in the iron foundries of Liverpool before becoming a force in the British Admiralty.

From the start, the Royal Geographical Society led the world in exploration, acting as patron and inspiration for the great expeditions to Africa, the Poles, and the Northwest Passage, that elusive sea connection between the Atlantic and Pacific. In the scramble to map the world, the society embodied the spirit of the age: that English exploration was a form of benign conquest.

The society's gold medal awards for feats of exploration read like a Who's Who of famous explorers, among them David Livingstone, for his 1855 explorations in Africa; the American explorer Robert Peary, for his 1898 discovery of the "northern termination of the Greenland ice"; Captain Robert Scott, the first Englishman to reach the South Pole, in 1912; and on and on.

Today the society's headquarters, housed in a red-brick Victorian lodge in South Kensington, still has the effect of a gentleman's club, with courteous staff, polished wood floors, and fine paintings.

AFTERWORD

The building archives the world's most important collection of private exploration papers, maps, documents, and artefacts. Among the RGS's treasures are the hats Livingstone and Henry Morton Stanley wore at their famous meeting ("Dr. Livingstone, I presume?") at Ujiji in 1871, and the chair the dying Livingstone was carried on during his final days in Zambia. The collection also includes models of expedition ships, paintings, dug-out canoes, polar equipment, and Charles Darwin's pocket sextant.

The library's 500,000 images cover the great moments of exploration. Here is Edmund Hillary's shot of Sherpa Tenzing standing on Everest. Here is Captain Lawrence Oates, who deliberately walked out of his tent in a blizzard to his death because his illness threatened to delay Captain Scott's party. Here, too is the American Museum of Natural History's 1920 expedition across the Gobi Desert in dusty convoy (the first to drive motorised vehicles across a desert).

The day I visited, curator Francis Herbert was trying to find maps for five different groups of adventurers at the same time from the largest private map collection in the world. Among the 900,000 items are maps dating to 1482 and ones showing the geology of the moon and thickness of ice in Antarctica, star atlases, and "secret" topographic maps from the former Soviet Union.

The mountaineer John Hunt pitched a type of base camp in a room at the RGS when he organised the 1953 Everest expedition that put Hillary and Tenzing on top of the world. "The society was my base, and source of my encouragement," said the late Lord Hunt, who noted that the nature of that work is different today from what it was when he was the society's president from 1976 to 1980. "When I was involved, there was still a lot of genuine territorial exploration to be done. Now, virtually every important corner—of the land surface, at any rate—has been discovered, and exploration has become more a matter of detail, filling in the big picture."

The RGS has shifted from filling in blanks on maps to providing a lead for the new kind of exploration, under the banner of geography: "I see exploration not so much as a question of 'what' and 'where' anymore, but 'why' and 'how': How does the earth work, the environment function, and how do we manage our resources sustainably?" says the society's director, Dr. Rita Gardner. "Our role today is to answer such questions at the senior level of scientific research," Gardner continues, "through our big, multidisciplinary expeditions, through the smaller expeditions we support and encourage, and by advancing the subject of geography, advising governments, and encouraging wider public understanding. Geography is the subject of the 21st century because it embraces everything—peoples, cultures, landscapes, environments— and pulls them all together."

The society occupies a unique position in world-class exploration. To be invited to speak at the RGS is still regarded as an accolade, the ultimate seal of approval of Swan, who in 1989 became the first person to walk to both the North and South Poles, and who says, "The hairs still stand on the back of my neck when I think about the first time I spoke at the RGS. It was the greatest honour."

The RGS set Swan on the path of his career as an explorer, assisting him with a 1979 expedition retracing Scott's journey to the South Pole. "I was a Mr. Nobody, trying to raise seven million dollars, and getting nowhere," says Swan. "The RGS didn't tell me I was mad—they gave me access to Scott's private papers. From those, I found fifty sponsors who had supported Scott, and persuaded them to fund me. On the basis of a photograph I found of one of his chaps sitting on a box of 'Shell Spirit,' I got Shell to sponsor the fuel for my ship."

The name "Royal Geographical Society" continues to open doors. Although the society's actual membership—some 12,600 "fellows," as they are called—is small, the organisation offers an incomparable net- work of people, experience, and expertise. This is seen in the work of the Expeditionary Advisory Centre. The EAC was established in 1980 to provide a focus for would-be explorers. If you want to know how to raise sponsorship, handle snakes safely, or find a mechanic for your trip across the Sahara, the EAC can help. Based in Lord Hunt's old Everest office, the EAC funds some 50 small expeditions a year and offers practical training and advice to hundreds more. Its safety tips range from the pragmatic—"In subzero temperatures, metal spectacle frames can cause frostbite (as can earrings and nose-rings)"—to the unnerving—"Remember: A decapitated snake head can still bite."

The EAC is unique, since it is the only centre in the world that helps small-team, low-budget expeditions, thus keeping the amateur—in the best sense of the word—tradition of exploration alive.

AFTERWORD

"The U.K. still sends out more small expeditions per capita than any other country," says Dr. John Hemming, director of the RGS from 1975 to 1996. During his tenure, Hemming witnessed the growth in exploration-travel. "In the 1960s we'd be dealing with 30 to 40 expeditions a year. By 1997 it was 120, but the quality hadn't gone down—it had gone up. It's a boom time for exploration, and the RGS is right at the heart of it."

While the EAC helps adventure-travellers, it concentrates its funding on scientific field research projects, mostly at the university level. Current projects range from studying the effect of the pet trade on Madagscar's chameleons, to mapping uncharted terrain in the south Ecuadorian cloud forest. Jen Hurst is a typical "graduate" of the EAC. With two fellow Oxford students, she received EAC technical training, support, and a $2,000 grant to do biological surveys in the Kyabobo Range, a new national park in Ghana.

"The RGS's criteria for funding are very strict," says Hurst. "They put you through a real grilling, once you've made your application. They're very tough on safety, and very keen on working alongside people from the host country. The first thing they wanted to be sure of was whether we would involve local students. They're the leaders of good practice in the research field."

When Hurst and her colleagues returned from Ghana in 1994, they presented a case study of their work at an EAC seminar. Their talk prompted a $15,000 award from the BP oil company for them to set up a registered charity, the Kyabobo Conservation Project, to ensure that work in the park continues, and that followup ideas for community-based conservation, social, and education projects are developed. "It's been a great experience, and crucial to the careers we hope to make in environmental work," says Hurst. "And it all started through the RGS."

The RGS is rich in prestige but it is not particularly wealthy in financial terms. Compared to the National Geographic Society in the U.S., the RGS is a pauper. However, bolstered by sponsorship from such companies as British Airways and Discovery Channel Europe, the RGS remains one of Britain's largest organisers of geographical field research overseas.

The ten major projects the society has undertaken over the last 20 or so years have spanned the world, from Pakistan and Oman to Brunei and Australia. The scope is large—hundreds of people are currently working in the field and the emphasis is multidisciplinary, with the aim to break down traditional barriers, not only among the different strands of science but also among nations. This is exploration as The Big Picture, preparing blueprints for governments around the globe to work on. For example, the 1977 Mulu (Sarawak) expedition to Borneo was credited with kick-starting the international concern for tropical rain forests.

The society's three current projects include water and soil erosion studies in Nepal, sustainable land use in Jordan, and a study of the Mascarene Plateau in the western Indian Ocean, to develop ideas on how best to conserve ocean resources in the future.

Projects adhere to a strict code of procedure. "The society works only at the invitation of host governments and in close co-operation with local people," explains Winser. "The findings are published in the host countries first, so they can get the benefit. Ours are long-term projects, looking at processes and trends, adding to the sum of existing knowledge, which is what exploration is about."

Exploration has never been more fashionable in England. More people are travelling adventurously on their own account, and the RGS's increasingly younger membership (the average age has dropped in the last 20 years from over 45 to the early 30s) is exploration-literate and able to make the fine distinctions between adventure / extreme / expedition / scientific travel.

Rebecca Stephens, who in 1993 became the first British woman to summit Everest, says she "pops along on Monday evenings to listen to the lectures." These occasions are sociable, informal affairs, where people find themselves talking to such luminaries as explorer Sir Wilfred Thesiger, who attended Haile Selassie's coronation in Ethiopia in 1930, or David Puttnam, who produced the film *Chariots of Fire* and is a vice president of the RGS. Shortly before his death, Lord Hunt was spotted in deep conversation with the singer George Michael.

Summing up the society's enduring appeal, Shane Winser says, "The Royal Geographical Society is synonymous with exploration, which is seen as something brave and exciting. In a sometimes dull, depressing world, the Royal Geographical Society offers a spirit of adventure people are always attracted to."

CHRONOLOGY

Circa 1 a.d. The first Bantu migration into Southeast Africa from the north begins. Indonesians begin settling the island of Madagascar.

1498   Portuguese explorer Vasco da Gama arrives at the site of modern-day Maputo, Mozambique.

1500   Portuguese explorer Diego Dias lands at Madagascar.

1855   Scottish missionary and explorer David Livingstone arrives at Victoria Falls on the River Zambezi.

1884-85 The Berlin West Africa Conference sets the stage for the European "scramble for Africa."

1891   Great Britain claims Rhodesia and the Lake Malawi (Lake Nyasa) area as protectorates. Portugal wins control of Mozambique.

1893   The territory of modern-day Malawi becomes the British Central Africa Protectorate. In 1907 its name will be changed formally to Nyasaland.

1896   After a failed rebellion by native peoples, Rhodesia is divided into northern and southern British protectorates. France formally makes Madagascar a colony.

1915   John Chilembwe leads a revolt in Nyasaland, opposing the mistreatment of black laborers.

1917   Activists rise up against the Portuguese regime in Mozambique over the conscription of Africans for service in World War I.

1946   Madagascar becomes a French territory, no longer a colony, acquiring a degree of self-control.

1951   Portugal makes Mozambique an overseas province.

1953   Great Britain unites Northern and Southern Rhodesia with Nyasaland into an unpopular confederation; the union is dissolved ten years later.

1960   Madagascar becomes a nation.

1962   The Frelimo movement is formed in Mozambique.

1964   Nyasaland becomes independent Malawi. Northern Rhodesia gains independence, becoming the Republic of Zambia. Southern Rhodesia's white leadership severs ties with Great Britain and declares an independent nation, triggering fifteen years of guerrilla warfare by black majority forces and international isolation.

CHRONOLOGY

In Mozambique, Frelimo militants launch a prolonged war against the Portuguese administration.

1966   Former nationalist leader Hastings Kamuzu Banda becomes president of Malawi; he will be proclaimed "president for life" in 1971.

1975   Mozambique gains independence from Portugal; Samora Machel becomes head of the new nation's communist government.

1980   Rhodesia's white minority leaders allow elections, effectively giving native Africans control of the country's parliament. Rhodesia becomes independent Zimbabwe.

1986   Mozambique President Samora Machel is killed in a plane crash; Joaquim Chissano succeeds him.

1990   A new constitution for Mozambique officially abandons fifteen years of socialist rule.

1992   Frelimo and Renamo forces in Mozambique sign an agreement ending more than fifteen years of civil war.

1997   Didier Ratsiraka, Madagascar's long-time head of state, again is elected president of the nation.

Late 2001   Zambia prepares for presidential elections.

GLOSSARY

abolitionist—a person who actively opposed slavery.

animist religion—a belief system holding that both helpful and evil spirits dwell in natural objects, including trees and stones.

apartheid—the system of government in South Africa that promoted racial segregation; it was in place from shortly after World War II until the black majority gained power in 1994.

charter colony—a colony run by a British chartered company rather than directly by the government.

deportation—the act of expelling someone from a country.

imperialist—a government official or other leader who advocates expanding the nation's influence by acquiring foreign territory.

plateau—a relatively flat, elevated land area.

poacher—a person who hunts or fishes on restricted property without permission.

rinderpest—a fatal cattle epidemic.

savannah—a broad, level, grassy area with scattered trees.

sisal—a fiber plant.

subsistence farming—growing enough food to feed the family or help supply the local village, not enough to export.

tribute—forced payment.

FURTHER READING

Barnes-Svarney, Patricia. *Zimbabwe*. ["Places and Peoples of the World" series] New York: Chelsea House Publishers. 1989.

Barrett, O.W. "Impressions and Scenes of Mozambique." *The National Geographic Magazine*, October 1910, p. 807.

Bessire, Mark. *Great Zimbabwe*. New York: Franklin Watts, a division of Grolier Publishing. 1998.

Blauer, Ettagale, and Jason Laur. *Madagascar: Enchantment of the World, Second Series*. New York: Children's Press, a division of Grolier Publishing. 2000.

Chater, Melville. "Rhodesia, The Pioneer Colony." *The National Geographic Magazine*, June 1935.

Davidson, Basil. *Modern Africa: A Social and Political History, Third Edition*. London: Longman Group UK Limited. 1994.

Davidson, Basil. *The Search for Africa: History, Culture, Politics*. New York: Random House. 1994.

Hallett, Robin. *Africa Since 1875: A Modern History*. Ann Arbor, MI: The University of Michigan Press. 1974.

Hargreaves, John D. *Decolonization in Africa*. London: Longman Group UK Limited. 1988.

Holmes, Timothy. *Zambia* ["Cultures of the World" series]. New York: Marshall Cavendish. 1998.

Hull, Richard W. *Southern Africa: Civilizations in Turmoil*. New York: New York University Press. 1981.

"Hunting Big Game in Portuguese East Africa," *The National Geographic Magazine*, November 1907, p. 723.

Kamm, Josephine. *Explorers Into Africa*. New York: Crowell-Collier Press [The Macmillan Company]. 1970.

Lauré, Jason, and Ettagale Blauer. *Mozambique*. ["Enchantment of the World" series] Chicago: Children's Press. 1995.

Mazrui, Ali A. *The Africans: A Triple Heritage*. Boston: Little, Brown and Company. 1986.

Moore, W. Robert. "Rhodesia, Hobby and Hope of Cecil Rhodes." *The National Geographic Magazine*, September 1944.

Outhwaite, Leonard. *Unrolling the Map: The Story of Exploration*. New York: John Day/Reynal and Hitchcock. 1935.

FURTHER READING

Packenham, Thomas. *The Scramble for Africa: 1876–1912*. New York: Random House. 1991.

Reader, John. *Africa: A Biography of the Continent*. New York: Alfred A. Knopf. 1998.

Sanders, Renfield. *Malawi* ["Places and Peoples of the World" series]. New York: Chelsea House Publishers. 1988.

Seaman, Louis Livingston. "The Wonders of the Mosi-Oa-Tunga: The Falls of the Zambesi." *The National Geographic Magazine*, June 1911, p. 561.

Shillington, Kevin. *Independence in Africa*. ["Causes and Consequences" series] Austin, TX: Steck-Vaughn Company. 1998.

Swingle, Charles F. "Across Madagascar by Boat, Auto, Railroad, and Filanzana." *The National Geographic Magazine*, August 1929, p. 178.

ABOUT THE AUTHORS

Dr. Richard E. Leakey is a distinguished paleo-anthropologist and conservationist. He is chairman of the Wildlife Clubs of Kenya Association and the Foundation for the Research into the Origins of Man. He presented the BBC-TV series *The Making of Mankind* (1981) and wrote the accompanying book. His other publications include *People of the Lake* (1979) and *One Life* (1984). Richard Leakey, along with his famous parents, Louis and Mary, was named by *Time* magazine as one of the greatest minds of the twentieth century.

Daniel E. Harmon is an editor and writer living in Spartanburg, South Carolina. The author of several books on history, he has contributed historical and cultural articles to *The New York Times, Music Journal, Nautilus,* and many other periodicals. He is the associate editor of *Sandlapper: The Magazine of South Carolina* and editor of *The Lawyer's PC* newsletter.

Deirdre Shields is the author of many articles dealing with contemporary life in Great Britain. Her essays have appeared in *The Times, The Daily Telegraph, Harpers & Queen*, and *The Field*.

INDEX

INDEX